Praise for Sympathy for the Drummer

"As succinct a definition of The Stones' magic as is possible to conjure … a marvellous, snare-crack of a book." —*Hot Press*

"Insightful, passionate, knowledgeable, funny, fresh and astute … *Sympathy for the Drummer* is hard to beat." —*International Times*

"An effusively infectious tribute to art in all of its myriad forms. Edison's insights into the Rolling Stones are backed up by a fluent scope of cultural historicity, and peppered with an array of no-nonsense broadsides. Compelling evidence to convince even the most non-partisan reader that Charlie is indeed the WORLD'S GREATEST ROCK'N'ROLL DRUMMER!" —**Jim Sclavunos**, Nick Cave and the Bad Seeds

"A verbal roller coaster ride through rock and roll, blues, jazz, drums, voodoo, sex, magic, and everything else that's truly important in life … jumps off the page, irresistible and infectious, and essential." —*Culture Sonar*

"Mike Edison's libertine prose swings and hits like Charlie Watt's right hand." —**Meredith Ochs**, author *Rock-and-Roll Woman*

"Exhilarating … magnificent insouciance …" —*Planet Rock*

"Utterly fascinating … Edison's words go way beyond the norm of rock and roll writing … it is impossible not to be moved by all Edison believes." —*Americana Highways* (**Book of the Year**)

"It's not hard to fathom why a former editor of both *Screw* and *High Times* magazines would find writing about the Rolling Stones, one of the most dissolute champions of sex and drugs, right in his conceptual wheelhouse. This book is a delightful look at the Stones through the eyes and the beats of their most reticent member. Finally someone gave this drummer some." —**Larry "Ratso" Sloman**, author *On the Road with Bob Dylan*

"A great voice of authority and knowledge, dispensed with free-wheeling fluidity. Super entertaining, and right on." —**Katherine Turman**, coauthor, *Louder Than Hell: The Complete Oral History of Heavy Metal*

"A wild ride through six-plus decades of music history. … An illuminating and massively entertaining book." —**Dan Epstein**, author *Big Hair and Plastic Grass*

"Edison is a gifted writer with a deft hand for making complex musical ideas relatable and enjoyable for the non-musician rock fan, and *Sympathy for the Drummer* is not just an interesting read, it's also often quite a funny one as well." —*The Recoup*

"Fanf**ckingtastic." —**Kenny Aranoff**

SYMPATHY FOR THE DRUMMER

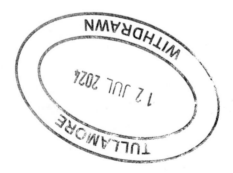

SYMPATHY FOR THE DRUMMER

WHY CHARLIE WATTS MATTERS

MIKE EDISON

Backbeat
Books

Backbeat Books
An imprint of The Rowman & Littlefield Publishing Group, Inc.
4501 Forbes Blvd., Ste. 200
Lanham, MD 20706
www.rowman.com

Distributed by NATIONAL BOOK NETWORK

Paperback edition published in 2021. Originally published
in hardcover by Backbeat Books in 2019.

Book design by Tom Seabrook
Cover photograph by Ethan Russell © Ethan Russell
Cover design and hand-lettering by Tilman Reitzle
Author photograph by Michael Lavine
Musical transcriptions by Kenny Aranoff, except "Rip This Joint" by Mike Edison
Uncredited photographs courtesy the author's personal collection

Library of Congress Cataloging-in-Publication Data available

ISBN 978-1-4930-5981-2 (paperback)
ISBN 978-1-4930-4773-4 (hardcover)
ISBN 973-1-4930-5069-7 (e-book)

♾™ The paper used in this publication meets the minimum requirements of
American National Standard for Information Sciences—Permanence of Paper for
Printed Library Materials, ANSI/NISO Z39.48-1992

"There is two kinds of music, the good, and the bad. I play the good kind."
LOUIS ARMSTRONG

"What the fuck's a rock drummer?"
CHARLIE WATTS

ALSO BY MIKE EDISON

NONFICTION

I Have Fun Everywhere I Go
Dirty! Dirty! Dirty!
You Are a Complete Disappointment

FICTION
Bye, Bye, Miss American Pie

CONTENTS

MICK
JAGGER

CHARLIE
WATTS

BRIAN
JONES

KEITH
RICHARD

BILL
WYMAN

Before the Revolution: the Rolling Stones doing their civic duty,
on the BBC's Juke Box Jury, *1964.* (Pictorial Press Ltd./Alamy)

Clyde of the rock'n'roll revolution. But the engine of the machine was the guy in back with the snare drum between his legs.

Keith was the best possible musical partner for Charlie Watts, with whom he created a conspiracy within a conspiracy. Together, they gave the Stones their unique swagger and flow—Keith's chopping rhythm guitar and preternatural sense for the riff pushed Charlie's sense of swing to the fore, forcing the run up to the beat and the gentle pulling back that became the Stones' signature style. And this is reason No. 1 Why Charlie Watts Matters—he understood better than anyone the difference between *anticipation* and *penetration*. He gave Keith Richards friction. He made Mick Jagger *explode*.

o o o

Charlie, Mick, and Keith were the Rolling Stones. Everyone else was replaceable.

Other members of the group have included Brian Jones, the founder of the group, a bluesman of no uncertain talent who had mastered the primitive urban spells of Elmore James and Slim Harpo, and who gave the band purpose, peeling off slide guitar riffs and harmonica stabs with a buttery ease. With Keith he began what famously became known as the "Ancient Art of Weaving," a sympathetic two-guitar relationship where rhythm and lead roles were cast to the side in favor of an organic stew where neither guitar dominated the soundscape. Later, Brian would expand his *grimoire* to include such exotica as dulcimer, marimba, and Mellotron. A beautiful man, music poured from his fingertips, and his contributions to the early Stones hits burned bright, until he burned out, a casualty of the lifestyle and the times in which he lived. He was asked unambiguously to leave the group in 1969, and was found dead in a swimming pool soon after, leaving a legion of broken hearts and an undying mystique.

Mick Taylor, Brian's replacement, was a horse of a different color, a lead guitar player who didn't weave so much as he rode on top of the rhythm section, and who would provide much of the stinging guitars and melodic aerodynamics across the Stones' run of classic records. This is when they first earned the title THE GREATEST ROCK'N'ROLL BAND IN THE WORLD, and there was no question, they were untouchable, the very best at what they did, the model for every band that came after them, in music, in fashion, in druggy behavior.

Taylor quit over some nonsense about not getting to write any songs, and seems to have regretted it ever since.

After a few auditions for the next guitar player, they landed on their old pal Ronnie Wood, ex of the Faces, themselves a somewhat sloppy version of the Stones, who fell-in with Keith almost too easily—Ronnie the rambunctious child, the optimist, the goofball, Keith the pirate who rarely traveled unarmed—and the Ancient Art of Weaving never sounded better.

Ronnie lasted longer than the last two guitar players put together, so maybe he was not actually replaceable, but seeing as he was in the band for twenty years before they made him a partner in the concern and not just an employee, you might surmise that the brain trust were hedging their bets. Occupational hazards in this group ran high.

Last but certainly not least of the Rolling Stones' official members was the severely underrated bassist Bill Wyman, whose accomplishments and presence have never been sung with as much praise as they merit. Often buried in the mix, he drove the band, playing with a very certain mastery of his instrument, and kept order in what could be an unruly mess. He was unequivocally a component part of the Stones' sound.

Bill's departure from the band was officially announced in 1993—he was fifty-six years old, and, after being in the band for thirty years or so, he seemed very happy for it. If he had left early on, who knows where the Stones might have drifted, but he was able to leave what he had created for the next cat, who plays wonderfully, but the blueprint was written long before he joined the team.

And there they are, the Rolling Stones. There have been keyboard players, and, more properly, pianists, at least one who got demoted on looks and not talent; a saxophone player who helped define their sound but got canned for filling a bathtub with Dom Pérignon—one toke over the line, even for the Rolling Stones; and a producer who helped them make the leap from juvenile delinquents to proper gangsters before flaming out on his own bad dope trip. It is a story as bold as Exodus or any of the Gospels, rife with fury and resurrection. And we'll get to all that.

But to the subject: Charlie Watts, an unrepentant jazz fan who had little love for rock'n'roll when he joined up with the Stones, and for whom drugs held little interest, found purchase in all of this. His ability to swing dirty blues, sleazy country music, and filthy hard rock with equal alacrity became the *sine qua non* of the organization. It only goes to follow that THE GREATEST ROCK'N'ROLL BAND IN THE WORLD could not exist without THE GREATEST ROCK'N'ROLL DRUMMER.

o o o

Much has been written about the Rolling Stones, much of it surrounding the enduring mystique of Mick and Keith, the drugs, the infighting, the women. There are angry feminist tracts and fawning puff pieces, critical essays, fan books, symphonies of yellow journalism, biographies, writs by producers and groupies and hangers on, and a book of wisdom compiled from excerpts of Keith's interviews. There are official coffee-table books, oral histories, and scads of photo books. Not content with being among the most documented human beings in history, several of them have written their own books to tell their side of the story.

The only thing they all seem to agree upon is that Charlie Watts motored this car. Keith has repeatedly said, "No Charlie, No Stones." And yet the literature surrounding Charlie Watts is anemic, a deficit in the landscape.

Perhaps this has much to do with Charlie's humility. Perhaps if he were more outspoken, less of a gentlemen, and played more like a lunatic than an actual *musician*; perhaps if his humor weren't so dry, if he were into drugs and sex and mayhem and didn't cast himself as the anti-rock star—married young, well mannered, and with little interest in the spotlight—perhaps if he drove cars into swimming pools and turned hotel rooms into kindling, then there would be a book or a movie about him. Perhaps if he shot lasers out of his eyes there would be an amusement-park ride.

But he was there for it all: the murder at Altamont, the myriad drug busts and casualties, the creation of some of the greatest musical documents of his time. His broken drum fills made good records great ones, and his toy drum set became the anchor for one of the most menacing, violent songs of all time. There was ancient wisdom in his rhythm, even as he found jazz in the most unlikely of all places—the most dangerous rock'n'roll band in the world.

He spent fifty years watching Mick Jagger shake his narrow ass across increasingly byzantine tours, and not only did he survive a lifetime on the road with Keith Richards, but together they became a beating heart, the greasiest, sexiest rhythm section in the history of the sport. Is there a band in the world not influenced in some way by the Rolling Stones?

I think it's time to give the drummer some.

Charlie Watts in New York City, 1964.
(Trinity Mirror/Mirrorpix/Alamy)

to Charles and Lillian. His old man was a lorry driver for the London, Midland and Scottish Railway.

More importantly, it was Gerry Mulligan's "Walkin' Shoes"—featuring Chico Hamilton's wickedly suave brush playing, along with Earl Bostic's version of "Flamingo," which was more like rhythm and blues than pure jazz—that was Charlie's radioactive spider, his gamma rays.

"Walkin' Shoes" swings easy, with none of the stomp that was the hallmark of the big-band era. It's groovy and catchy, sexy, teasing, but not obviously exciting. The drums are unhurried. It is *cool*, not *hot*. Charlie says he first heard it when he was thirteen, and it was soon after that he took the strings off of a banjo and had at it with his own set of brushes.

Charlie never took drum lessons. When he was still at it a year later, his dad, in an act of wild abandon and selflessness that would change the course of popular music, bought him a second-hand drum set.

Charlie was also an aspiring graphic designer, an art-school student who by graduation had already begun to climb the corporate advertising ladder. He was going to be a success no matter what, but preferred to play the drums, even as his straight gig was beginning to pay dividends. He sat in playing Monk and modern stuff in coffee shops here and there, and had a run at playing in a bar mitzvah band—a bit of a stretch, but he always said he could cover it if the piano player knew his shit—but the main thing was, the cat *loved* jazz, and he *loved* to play the drums.

Sure, lots of guys would rather play music than work in an

office, but how many of them are going to have the mettle to make that choice? I've known lots of guys who quit playing to become *dentists*, but then again, I'm pretty sure their lives are much better for it. Certainly the world is a better place for their sacrifice.

Charlie, too, it should be noted, scoured *DownBeat* magazine not just for hip sounds from the New World but for sartorial flare. Those jazz cats knew how to dress, and somewhere along the line he had figured out that to *sound good*, you had to *look good*, and he always rode on that fine edge. Sure, years later he might make the gig in a Stones T-shirt (and there was no telling what sort of frock Mick might arrive in), but you try playing that set in a suit and tie. For a while, in the 1970s, Charlie was a perennial on "best drummers" lists. By the beginning of the next century, he was not only being celebrated for his drumming but appearing on "best dressed" lists with accompanying features in posh rags—the kind that smell good, like *Vanity Fair* and *Gentlemen's Quarterly*. The die of Charlie's fate, it would seem, had been cast. Whereas some heroes had strength far beyond those of mortal men, Charlie knew how to swing. He was urbane. Lots of guys had cool clothes, Charlie had *zork*.

° ° °

When Charlie was first coming up, the whole of jazz drumming had already been architected by a race of supermen with names like Papa Jo Jones and Philly Joe Jones—the former best known for his work with the Count Basie Orchestra, the latter for his time with Miles Davis—and this is the root of Charlie's powers, a torrent of dotted eighth notes and triplets that could propel the song without needless clutter.

Given the chance, Charlie will effuse like a child on a sugar high about his heroes, Sid Catlett and Dave Tough, all-but forgotten big-band drummers of the 1930s. He speaks in awe of a time when 52nd Street in New York was a mecca for jazz. While another generation spoke of missing out on Hendrix at Woodstock or Zeppelin at the Forum, Charlie's dream was to go to see Ellington at the Cotton Club up in Harlem, Louis Armstrong at the Roseland in Chicago, or Charlie Parker anywhere.

Looking good in Germany, 1965. (Hermann Schröer/Timeline Images/Alamy)

Such was Charlie Watts's love of Charlie Parker that he wrote a children's book about him when he was just starting his career as an artist and designer in 1960—*Ode to a High Flying Bird.* "He'd often hear his friends raving and chirping about the scene in New York," Charlie (Parker, that is) says to his other bird friends, as he "flew from his nest in Kansas City, bound for New York." *High Flying Bird* would make a comeback in 1991, when Charlie, now an accidental rock star, made a record out of it, *From One Charlie.* And this, too, is another reason Why Charlie Watts Matters: he was always true to his school. Even under the weight of the Rolling Stones, the jazz never left.

He was gonzo for bebop pioneers Max Roach, Kenny Clarke, and Roy Haynes, hot jazz icons Chick Webb and Baby Dodds, and later Tony Williams—a thoroughly original talent with intimidating cymbal technique, who was hired by Miles Davis when he was just a teenager—and Elvin Jones, whose influence was far more applicable and evident in the hands of Jimi Hendrix's perfectly expressionist drummer, Mitch Mitchell, than it could ever be in the hard jump and swing of Charlie Watts. Which is another reason Why Charlie Watts Matters: he always knew what to bring to work, and what to leave at home.

When Charlie first had the bright idea to play the drums, there wasn't a drummer alive who wasn't directly influenced by Gene Krupa. Krupa was the "King of Swing," and the man who more than anyone made the drummer a star. When he hit the drum solo in "Sing, Sing, Sing" with Benny Goodman's Orchestra in 1937, audiences lost their shit. When Krupa played that drum boogie, he made the drums *roar*. Never before had such a primal rhythm dominated the big-band stage. It was musical, and it *rolled*. It lived between the jungle and the ballroom. It was rock'n'roll, when "rock and roll" was still just a fuck euphemism.[3]

---

3 The phrase "rock and roll" was a bit of poetry born of sea shanties, the motion of ships on the ocean. But sailors being sailors, it quickly became a euphemism for the thing with two heads, the thing with a thousand euphemisms. It was also embraced in spirituals and gospel songs, as in "rocking and rolling … in the arms of Moses," but it wasn't long before it showed up on a "race" record, Trixie Smith's 1922 "My Man Rocks Me (With One Steady Roll)," generally credited with being the first record to put it over for what it was. There's more to the story, of course, but you get the gist.

It was also the beginning of the modern drum solo, and, as such, has probably done as much harm as good, because, let's face it, there have only been a few good drum solos in the history of the game—Krupa on "Sing, Sing, Sing," Joe Morello's time-melting break on Dave Brubeck's "Take Five," "Wipe Out" by the Surfaris (drums by the unsung Ron Wilson), and "Moby Dick," John Bonham's colossal Led Zeppelin centerpiece. The lion's share of the rest are what I'd call "extra-musical affairs," largely show-business nonsense, all of the wondrous, musical things played by Max Roach, and the sensational excesses of Buddy Rich notwithstanding.[4]

But that is a discussion for another time. For now, let's just be happy that the Rolling Stones were smart enough to hire a jazz cat who would always put the *roll* in front of the *rock*, a guy who didn't measure his worth by how many notes he played, whose ego was tempered by the primacy of his job: to put the *song* over, to make the *band* sound great. While others battled their drums, Charlie finessed his. He knew when to swing, he knew when to stomp. Charlie didn't play drum solos, not because he wasn't good enough to play them, but because he was good enough not to have to.

---

4 "Moby Dick" is the logical extension of all of this, based largely on Max Roach's "The Drum Also Waltzes" and combining the crazy syncopation of Krupa and the driving force of "Wipe Out" with Buddy Rich's incredible technical power. Bonham was also, like Charlie Watts, a huge fan of Joe Morello, from whom he got the idea to play the drums with his hands. Incidentally, part of the beauty of the "Take Five" solo is that Morello unleashes it while the piano is still vamping and marking time for him, which is the way more drum solos ought to be. When the guitar player is playing a solo, the band doesn't normally stop and leave the stage, right?

The sensational Little Richard, 1957.
(Michael Ochs Archives/Getty Images)

more effete affair)—you were hearing the sound of New Orleans bubbling up through the amphetamine daze of the Star-Club in Hamburg, where the Beatles had cut their teeth.

Charlie, for his part, would largely find the mojo for his gig in the Rolling Stones in Chicago's South Side, and especially on the records issued on the Chess label by Muddy Waters, Bo Diddley, Howlin' Wolf, and Chuck Berry.

The best Chicago drummers knew how to cook the tempos low and slow, and swing with precision. They could also roll and tumble and hot up any house party. They were masters of the Hypnotic Shuffle and the Big Beat. The Latin Groove was never too far away. And in the most profound blues, the deep Delta sway of Muddy and Wolf, they could bend time, hovering above the beat the same way Michael Jordan seemed to defy gravity by hovering in the air when he took a jump shot.

Clifton James was Bo Diddley's main man, and, along with legendary maracas player Jerome Green, they built the Bo Diddley beat from the ground up, the two of them coming together and forming something like one gigantic super drummer.[6]

---

6 DO NOT UNDERESTIMATE THE IMPORTANCE OF THE MARACAS, OR THE MARACAS PLAYER. First of all, do you have any idea how hard it is to find a dedicated maracas player, a guy or gal who is happy just to play the maracas, without the ego of having to be the big dog on the drum kit? Never mind that, do you have any idea how hard it is to play the maracas accurately? They have to play solid time with the drums and *against* the guitar, or with the guitar and *against* the drums, for that is the true secret of the Bo Diddley rhythm, like so much else: *friction*. Also, try to play the maracas with Bo Diddley for forty straight minutes without having a heart attack. Serious maracas-playing is dangerous territory.

Bo's music was ferocious—it wasn't linked to jump blues and swing or straight blues changes as much as it was all about the purity of *the beat*. Bo was both futuristic and primitive, plying space-age sounds of profound reverb and tremolo against rhythms that were yanked straight out of Africa and spiked with the Spanish tinge.[7] It was true jungle music, every song a sex bomb.

But of all the heroes on the Chess label, it was Chuck Berry's stamp that could be felt most indelibly on the Rolling Stones, who worshipped him relentlessly.[8] Obviously ground zero for Keith's guitar style, Chuck also had some viciously good drummers coming in and out of his band.

Ebby Hardy, Chuck's first drummer, was not pretty—he horrified crowds with his snaggletooth grin—but he was a jazzer of profound looseness and flow who would later confound Charlie Watts, as he would anyone who tried to cover his shit. On the records he made with Chuck Berry, his drumming was just too groovy and too far out to copy. Songs like "Come On" and "Bye Bye Johnny," both covered by the Stones, seemed to roll in some alternate universe—another dimension where the bayou met the bright lights of downtown St. Louis, and where the drums were unrestrained by the normal rules of gravity.

---

7 What jazz avatar Jelly Roll Morton called the fundamental Latin, Afro-Cuban rhythm: "If you can't manage to put tinges of Spanish in your tunes," Morton would say, "you will never be able to get the right seasoning, I call it, for jazz."

8 Should also be noted that, as the Stones did, Chuck "worshipped" Muddy Waters—Chuck called him "the greatest inspiration in the launching of my career." It's a strong lineage.

drums on "Johnny B. Goode" *swung* with the syncopation of jazz and the big bands, even as the guitar played *straight eights*, which was the future of rock. It was a sophisticated approach—if everyone played *on the beat*, it would have sounded *monolithic*, all *rock* and no *roll*, and then where would we have been?[9]

You can blame it on every shitty white blues band in the world that feels like they must *rock out* with the syncopation removed like dead bodies from a crime scene, or a million wedding bands that just aren't good enough to keep the jazz in those songs alive. Or, you can just blame it on the Beatles, whose version of "Roll Over Beethoven" is giddy and wonderful, but without much in the swing department.

And it wasn't just Chuck Berry who got rooked on the deal. The Doors diminished the power of Howlin' Wolf's trenchant, harrowing, and subversively sexual "Back Door Man" so thoroughly that they should have been shipped to Chicago and given heart transplants. Their Bo Diddley was even worse.

By the mid-1960s, things were taking a nasty turn: the idea that it was easy to play this shit had taken hold.

In a fundamental way, blues is like pizza—it has few ingredients, and yet it is astonishing how many people fuck it up. You can bend the "pizza" to your will, as Charles Mingus and Ornette Coleman and Iggy Pop and Captain Beefheart and a few others have done, but you cannot change the fact that you are going to need some dough, cheese, and tomatoes to get started, and yes, I know there

---

9 Well, the Ramones figured it out, but such was their beauty. Not everyone could be a successful cubist, either.

Stones circa 1963. NB Ian Stewart, top right, with maracas. (Photofest)

are white pies and clam pies and *pizza rosso senza formaggio*, but that doesn't mean that it is a delivery system for your foolishness, either—you put pineapple on it, and it dies. And no matter the technology of the day, you're going to need an oven, ideally one that burns fuel culled from the earth, like wood or coal.

When Jim Morrison sang about a "back beat that was narrow and hard to master," he might as well have been making excuses for his own drummer. No matter their superstar pop status and counterculture bona fides, their Living Theater pretensions and lysergic distractions, at the bottom of it all, the Doors represented the worst sort of rock mendacity: a blues band that could not play the blues.

It was like an epidemic where the simple but hard-learned lessons in blues learned by Brian, Keith, Charlie, and Mick were wiped out by a single novel pathogen, namely rock-star egos.

While the Doors were busy neutering "Back Door Man," Cream were mercilessly horse-whipping "Spoonful"—one of Howlin' Wolf's most meditative and darkest numbers, a one-chord modal tone poem dedicated to murder and drugs and love and money. In the hands of Eric Clapton, Jack Bruce, and Ginger Baker, it took off into a high-flying but ultimately thoughtless vehicle for their individual egos, a twenty-minute jam that at times wasn't much more than atonal cacophony—not necessarily a bad thing, if you were John Coltrane or Cecil Taylor, but Cream were not John Coltrane or Cecil Taylor. So great was their individual indulgence that at times they were not even playing together; bassist Jack Bruce has said that there were plenty of times when they were not listening to each other, and guitarist Eric Clapton has joked about at least one night when he stopped playing and no one in the band even noticed.[10] With "Spoonful," they successfully stomped the *roll* out of the damn thing, leaving nothing but the false promises of *rock*, and begging the musical question: *Couldn't they have just as easily found a different chord, and left this one the hell alone?*

The damage they did can still be felt.

---

10 More proof that tragedy plus time equals comedy.

Is it ironic, then, that in 1962, four years before he became the overpowering drummer for Cream, Ginger Baker was an incredibly gifted but traditional jazz drummer when he got the call to join Alexis Korner's Blues Incorporated, replacing Charlie Watts, who had already lowered his own expectations of playing jazz to play the blues?

Alexis Korner was the king of a small but fertile British blues scene in 1962, a hub of musicians that included Ian Stewart, Brian Jones, Jack Bruce, and Charlie Watts, and fans that included John Mayall, Jimmy Page, Eric Clapton, and Rod Stewart, not to mention the other Rolling Stones, who by then had already formed their first lineup, and were about to find themselves to be the beaus of the ball.[11]

"We were really lacking a good drummer. We were really feeling it," Keith later told the curiously named *Rolling Stone* magazine. "The R&B thing started to blossom, and we found playing on the bill with us in a club, there were two bands on. Charlie was in the other band ... we did our set and Charlie was knocked out

---

11 This story has been told in great detail many times, how school chums Mick and Keith reconnected by chance at Dartford rail station and made a love connection built on the Chuck Berry and Muddy Waters records Mick had tucked under his arm, and how they were soon forming a band with Ian Stewart (a boogie-woogie piano player who would be nudged out of the band the second they had a taste of popularity because *he didn't look like a Rolling Stone*, although they kept him around to play piano and load the van, as needed), and Dick Taylor (later of the insanely good Pretty Things), Brian Jones (the spiritual force of the operation), and a drummer who was not Charlie Watts. They made their debut with their first steady lineup in 1963.

by it. 'You're great, man,' he says, 'but you need a fucking good drummer.' So we said, 'Charlie, we can't afford you, man.' [But] he said OK and told the other band to fuck off, 'I'm gonna play with these guys.' That was it. When we got Charlie, that really made it for us. We started getting a lot of gigs."

And that's where their career trajectories overlapped for one hot second, Charlie Watts and Ginger Baker. Ginger would soon be lauded as some sort of drumming superhero, while Charlie went about his business, keeping the *roll* in the Rolling Stones, with little if any fanfare.

There have been other great minimalists in our culture: Coco Chanel leaps to mind, also Monk, Miles Davis, the Ramones, Keith Richards, and the great drummers of Chess Records, all of whom matter because they proved that less is so often more than more.

Best seat in the house. British television, 1965.
(Cyrus Andrews/Michael Ochs Archive/Getty Images)

THREE

NOT FADE AWAY

SOME DRUMMERS ARE BORN WITH GREAT TASTE, others achieve great taste, and others have great taste thrust upon them. Charlie hit the trifecta.

When Charlie joined the Stones, he was still an unrepentant jazzer. "Charlie had come to rhythm and blues because of his jazz connection," Keith recalls in his extraordinary memoir, *Life*, "but he had not got rock and roll down at the time. I wanted him to hit a little harder. He was still too jazz for me. We knew he was a great drummer, but in order to play with the Stones, Charlie studied Jimmy Reed and Earl Phillips."

Reed, an obsessive love interest of Brian Jones and Keith Richards, was the master of the laid-back shuffle, and his drummer, Earl Phillips, practically seditious in his understated pulse. His songs were deceptively simple but nearly impossible to cop, not if you wanted to get it right—Phillips's gigantic backbeat and soft shuffles on "Honest I Do," "Big Boss Man," "Bright Lights Big City," and "Baby What You Want Me to Do" gave Reed an incalculable sort of swing, haunting, but with no uncertain drive.[1]

Jimmy Reed, the King of Anticipation.
(Vee Jay Records publicity photo)

Like most of the great Chicago bluesmen, Reed was born in Mississippi and took with him the swampy, ambient haze of the Delta, but unlike Muddy or Wolf, he shed the rougher, more rural notes and added a lithe jazz to his sound. It's no wonder that Charlie, too, fell in love with him. He saw what a lot of less humble cats would have sniffed at, telling DownBeat that "Keith and Brian taught me, through constant playing of Jimmy Reed. Reed and his drummer, Earl Phillips, were as sensitive as Paul Motian with Bill Evans." Later, he would add that Phillips was one of the great jazz drummers—a ridiculous thing to say, if you were a snob, that is, but Charlie was never one of *those* jazz fans. And this is yet one more reason Why Charlie

---

1 Phillips's shuffles are mesmerizing, not only on Jimmy Reed's records, but also occasionally with king of the primitive modernists, John Lee Hooker, and many others, but most notably on some of Howlin' Wolf's most hypnotic meditations—"Evil," "Smokestack Lighting," and the indomitable "Forty-Four," with its heavy accent on "the one."

Watts Matters, because he knew that the real magic lived in the heart, and not in the hands.[2]

The tempos of those Jimmy Reed songs are maddening—there seems to be an extra breath between the downbeat on the bass drum and the upbeat on the snare, and yet it all falls together, it *swings*, it doesn't lurch or stumble, it is exactly the kind of thing that drives drummers to insanity. Which is why most of them avoid it—it is far more difficult to play slow than fast. It isn't just the notes you don't play, it is the space between the ones that you do. A lot of cats have no idea what to do with space—all they can do is poop in it. It's hard for young musicians to understand— *sometimes you just gotta lay off-a that thang*. Sinatra knew it, and

---

2 There were a lot of blues drummers cutting it in Chicago and percolating up into the Charlie Watts ozone, and it would be a shame not to mention at least a few of them. Odie Payne, another Knapp School grad, master bluesman, and Chess Studio regular who came into Chuck's band later on and played on "You Never Can Tell," "Promised Land," and "Nadine," but made his bones early on with Elmore James (another Brian Jones obsession—Brian began his career calling himself "Elmo Lewis" in tribute), playing on one of the most iconic blues sides of all time, "Dust My Broom," not to mention "The Sky Is Crying," "It Hurts Me, Too," "Shake Your Money Maker," and on and on. Odie later spent most of his time across town working for the Cobra label and West Side blues wizards Otis Rush and Magic Sam, both covered by the Stones on their twenty-first-century cover disc, *Blue & Lonesome*. Francis Clay, another jazzer who played with Charlie Parker before he found his way into Muddy's band (no wonder Charlie Watts loved him) is probably best known for cutting the jumpin' "I Got My Mojo Workin'." And the tom-tom combusting Frank Kirkland, who along with Clifton James, was one of Bo Diddley's original drummers, playing on many of his greatest hits and frequently traveling with the band. He also swung like Tarzan with one of my favorites, the lesser-known, fez-wearing slide guitar ace, J. B. Hutto.

the Stones knew it, and that's why they got the girls.

The Stones were so confident in their approach to this impossible music that they would often open up their early gigs with a swanky Jimmy Reed number. This would change later, of course, when they started playing to bigger crowds and came out of the gate swinging for the fences,[3] but for now, I think it would be nice to take a moment to admire their confidence and uncommon faith in their drummer to come out in front of a bunch of screaming teenagers and lay this kind of unhurried groove on them. They didn't *pander*, they *seduced*. *Anticipation*, not *penetration*.

○ ○ ○

For all of their blues priapism—Brian Jones was especially dogmatic when it came to playing blues and R&B over tawdry rock'n'roll— the first Rolling Stones single was a Chuck Berry cover, and a lousy one at that.

In 1963, the star sign of rock'n'roll was Beatles, with Beatles Ascending, a cosmic occurrence announced gleefully with the *boom-didda-bop-bop* tom-tom tattoo that Ringo peels off at the beginning of "She Loves You." Great bit of drumming, that.

Within a year, the Beatles would be everything, and everything would be coming up Beatles. As for the Stones, they were still just

---

3 But they never strayed too far, bringing back Reed's "The Sun Is Shining" for their free concert at Altamont in 1969 (sandwiched between the much darker numbers "Sympathy for the Devil" and "Stray Cat Blues"), and recording his punishing "Little Rain" for their later blues album, *Blue & Lonesome*, in 2016. And yet there are those who still say you can never come home…

primitives, but with a will to walk erect. One reviewer at the time called them "five awesome apes who perpetrate awesome musical onslaughts."

The single, "Come On," was the idea of manager/producer Andrew Loog Oldham, who wanted to push them into more commercial territory, and somehow it came out all Mersey Beaten and sugar sweet, Ebby Hardy's spectacular, rollicking explosion of jazz and rhythm rolled over and flattened.

Mick Jagger called the record "shit," and as a group they refused to play it live, so potent was their enmity for it. But it sold enough to hit No. 21 on the UK charts, a breezy hundred thousand copies, and got them on a tour with their hero, Bo Diddley.

It's hard to imagine such a thing—the Stones opening up for Bo Diddley, not to mention Little Richard, who joined the tour after half a dozen dates. It was a package show, and the Stones were allotted ten minutes to play, ten minutes to get their kit off and create pandemonium.[4] Typical set: "Money," "Poison Ivy," "Fortune Teller," "Route 66," and a Chuck Berry number that wasn't their single, e.g. "Roll Over Beethoven" or "Memphis, Tennessee." They were on their way, THE GREATEST GARAGE BAND IN THE WORLD!

More importantly, Keith and Charlie and Mick got to watch Bo Diddley every night, and they *learned*, boy-oh-boy did they *learn*.

Bo Diddley was not only the progenitor of a primordial African

---

4 The Everly Brothers were the other big act on a show that featured a comedian, Brit singer Julie Grant, soon-to-be-forgotten band the Flintstones, pop singer and soon-to-be producer to the stars Mickie Most, and of course Little Richard, Bo Diddley, and the Rolling Stones.

Ahead of their time: Bo Diddley, the Duchess, and Jerome Green. (Pictorial Press Ltd./Alamy)

swamp-rock and futurist blues, he was a pimp-rollin' mutherfucker whose songs oozed with the stank of sweat and sex, his hypermodern wash of rhythm guitar playing, his tropical boogie, his explosive shimmy and shake, all a potent mating call that seemed to draw its power from ancient fertility gods, space aliens, and John the Conqueror root. He was also a genius at good old-fashioned show business.

That the other guitar player in his band, the Duchess, was a statuesque woman of startling pulchritude, charm, and talent did not hurt the act. Nor did her skintight, gold lamé catsuit and custom Gretsch guitar, a six-string showstopper with Cadillac fins.

Bo was way ahead of his time, employing female guitar players, and not just for stage dressing—before the Duchess (Norma-Jean Wofford) joined the fray, Lady Bo (Peggy Jones) filled that spot, and she could go toe to toe with Bo not only in provocative moves but in righteous goddam guitar playing, doing the Ancient Art of Weaving with the man himself.

It was unheard of in the late 1950s and early 1960s for women to be rocking onstage with the men. The best of the day were the great girl groups, the Shirelles and the Ronettes, and none of them were weaponized with electric guitars. This was exactly the strain of primal Negro eroticism that Mick and Keith mainlined, at least until the drugs took over.

And that beat, oh, that *beat!*

○ ○ ○

When the Stones got back from that tour, they dropped their second single, a hand-me-down ditty from their friends John Lennon and Paul McCartney, "I Wanna Be Your Man." It did a little better than "Come On," but despite Brian Jones's best efforts to dirty it up with some slide guitar, it was still far too sweet for boys who yearned to be men.

The third single, however, was the charm—the Buddy Holly

cover "Not Fade Away," which climbed all the way to No. 3 in the UK and dented the US charts at No. 48, driven by Charlie's wicked Bo Diddley beat. This is what it sounded like:

SEX!

Sex!

SEX!

SEX! SEX!

They had learned well. They even got the maracas right, rubbing up against the drums, giving it the friction of anticipation, and Mick pulling no punches:

> *I'm gonna tell you how it's gonna be,*
> *You're gonna give your love to me.*

It was licentious, bordering on lewd. And it's an odd phenom— so often people listen to their *memories* and not the *actual music*, and they remember *wrong*. It's an easy trap to fall in to. You might recall the original version being a rocker, if so, but your memory has been diddled by the Rolling Stones, who turned the song from teenage heart-throb into a troglodytic soundtrack for caveman romance, and set the standard for every other cover version that followed.[5]

---

5 Incidentally, Canadian prog-fantasy band Rush chose "Not Fade Away" for their first single, although they were arguably a much different band in 1973, before drummer Neil Peart came on board and helped chart their future. Short of the

Buddy Holly's original recording of "Not Fade Away" was a laid-back affair, not a boisterous rocker. Flowers and candy, not a psychosexual demand. Jerry Allison, Buddy Holly's drummer, was one of the very best in the business, a picture of humility who could throw down handclaps or a slammin' backbeat, whatever the song needed. "Peggy Sue" was his most spectacular outing, a free and easy flow of paradiddles—*right, left, right, right, left, right, left, left*—tribal and groovy, and the kind of flawless rudimental technique that one hardly ever sees in rock drumming. He had the smoothness and flow of Joe Morello or Gene Krupa, and never overplayed, even as the song seemed to be built from the drums up.

Charlie was huge on Jerry Allison. "He doesn't really play the drums," he has said. "He plays the songs, and that is really more important within the context of that music. If you're playing to a songwriter, that's much more important than having all the technique in the world."[6]

Allison was also a decent thumper. So much that when it came to recording "Not Fade Away," his Bo Diddley beat was far too heavy for Holly's light touch, threatening to bury the saccharine, Jordanaires-esque background vocals, and lay waste to Holly's

complex arrangements and polished technique that would become their hallmark, this first single sounds like an ad for an amusement park or a sugary breakfast cereal. It is little wonder they decided to abandon the blues and go for sci-fi and progressive rock—it was easier to play.

6 Big-band artifact Buddy Rich, often celebrated as "the world's greatest drummer," didn't see it that way, once proclaiming, "I think the drummer should sit back there and play some drums and never mind the tunes, just get up there and wail."

hugs'n'kisses good vibe. Allison wound up playing the part by tapping on cardboard boxes.

Even so, the rhythm was impeccable. Allison's melodic sense, his belief in the song, put him in the same category with Max Roach and Levon Helm, two drummers who would elevate the role of the drum set by getting inside the song—Roach as a progenitor of bebop, and Helm, in roots-rock avatars the Band, as the greatest singing drummer ever, able to back up his most nuanced vocal phrasing note-for-note by playing the melody, proving that *if you were playing the melody, you didn't have to count.* It seemed perfectly natural, but not one in a hundred drummers could pull it off.

And it was with this gust of a tailwind, a hit record boasting "love bigger than a Cadillac"—which sounds a lot filthier in Mick's mouth than it ever would have coming from Buddy Holly—the Rolling Stones tootled off to conquer America.

o o o

It was a crappy tour. Eleven gigs, rife with chaos, and, when they made their American TV debut, they had to suffer the idiocy of Dean Martin. At least on that trip they got to fulfill a dream: they got to record at Chess Records in Chicago and meet Muddy Waters, who legendarily was up on a ladder painting the ceiling when the Stones walked in, and without fanfare told them he dug what they were doing with his music. Muddy, another cat who had no time for inflated egos. Later, he'd help them haul some amplifiers out of a car.

When the tour was over, they hung out at the Apollo Theater, watching James Brown, who was there for a week, doing five shows a day.

Let that sink in: *a week of James Brown, five shows a day.*

Charlie spent some time at the Apollo with Mick and Keith, but, true to his school, he also went off the reservation and cruised the jazz clubs of Manhattan and got to see Miles Davis with Tony Williams. He saw Gene Krupa, Earl Hines, Max Roach's wicked hard-bop group with Sonny Rollins, and Mingus with Dannie Richmond on drums, which at its most fevered pitch sounded like Ray Charles gone 'round the bend.

Mingus was a magician who never let go of his blues and gospel roots. Of all of these giants, it may be that Mingus and Richmond—whom he would see many times—had the greatest latent effect on Charlie's playing, whether he realized it or not. Mingus's band could come awfully close to rock'n'roll, and when the Stones began to explode in the late 1960s and early 1970s, you could hear distant but sympathetic vibrations of Mingus's own blues free-for-alls in the surging, stop-time shuffle bits that took off on "Midnight Rambler" and the loosest bits of *Exile on Main St.*

Meanwhile, James Brown gave Mick lots of tips about the business, and Mick paid him back by swiping his best dance moves. By the time the Stones got back to the States later that year, Mick was doing James Brown's shimmy and the Stones were feuding with him about who had to play before whom at a TV taping. This was all part of the Stones' evolution—lessons and attitude learned firsthand from the gods of jazz and R&B, knowledge far more valuable than any silk from the orient.

The next year, when they appeared on the American TV show *Shindig!*, they demanded, like blues terrorists, that either Muddy or Howlin' Wolf appear with them. Wolf made the gig, and they sat, quite literally, at his feet, like some sort of Hillel Academy for twenty-something blues scholars.

o o o

When the Stones made their first American television appearance, in 1964, on the *Hollywood Palace* show hosted by Dean Martin, they delivered their own hotted-up version of "I Just Want to Make Love to You."[7]

It was very clear that Rolling Stones did not want to hold your

---

7 It should be noted that this, like many of the best songs recorded at Chess Records, was penned by the great Willie Dixon, a songwriter of such power as to lay claim to his own Great American Songbook, right up there with Gershwin, Porter, or Berlin: he is largely responsible for the vast repertoire of blues songs perfected in Chicago and later adopted with various degrees of success by tawdry rock musicians. A few of his better known numbers among the five hundred he wrote include "Hoochie Coochie Man," "Wang Dang Doodle," "Bring It on Home," "Evil," "I Ain't Superstitious," "Little Red Rooster," "Spoonful," "You Shook Me," "I Can't Quit You Baby," and "Whole Lotta Love," which he "co-wrote" with Led Zeppelin, meaning they coughed up a songwriting credit after they got caught boosting his song "You Need Love" and were summarily sued for their carelessness. It also should be mentioned that the man was a powerhouse on bass, one of the best ever, and helped drive Chuck and Bo and Muddy and Wolf on most of their records, and deserves credit as much or more than anyone for being the mastermind behind the classic Chicago blues sound. But you already knew that.

hand. They weren't interested in any fumbling petting. They didn't want you to cook or clean. They didn't even care who else you were fucking.

I don't want you to be true,
I just want to make love to you

It was what you'd call "on-message." There is something very powerful about announcing one's intentions.

When Muddy cut it with Fred Below on drums, it was all foreplay. Even Little Walter's wildly distorted harp, which sounded like a jet airplane landing next to you in bed, took its sweet goddam time about it. When the Stones jacked up the tempo and injected it with the Spanish tinge, it was still unmistakably about *anticipation—nervous anticipation*, but anticipation nonetheless, and, if anything, it felt like it might explode *too soon*. It was something every teenager could understand.

It was *Diddleyfied* and *Muddied*, it was *swingin'* and it was *stompin'*, it was *rock* and it was *roll*. You could hear in every thump and thwack exactly why they wanted and needed Charlie—his swinging pulse was unsafe at any speed.

Dean wasn't too thrilled. It's likely he didn't even bother to listen. "Aren't they great," he slurred drunkenly after they played, throwing a huge, sarcastic eye-roll toward the ceiling.

Dean was a dinosaur, soon to be extinct, and when it came to this modern rock music he was like his pal Sinatra, too cool for the new school. He made a few drunken jokes about long hair, and then drooled into his drink, three sheets to the wind. "I've been rolled while I was stoned," he guffawed. Big laughs.

Dean Martin was a jerk. Maybe somebody, somewhere thought he was a likeable drunk, but seriously, *who insults their guests like that?* What kind of asshole has young musicians on their TV show, *and then mocks them?* Such was the entertainment establishment. *Frightened.* He should have been—he came very close to spending the rest of his life with a guitar-shaped dent in his skull, thanks to Keith.

Bob Dylan wrote *"dean martin should apologize t' the rolling stones"* in the liner notes to *Another Side of Bob Dylan,* released that summer—because in 1964, the cardboard sleeve of a twelve-inch long-playing phonograph record was an expedient method of communicating outrage. It was an odd time, indeed. Everything seemed about to explode.

o o o

When the Stones came back to the States a few months later, they made their debut on *The Ed Sullivan Show.* He was equally appalled.

When the Beatles first appeared on *The Ed Sullivan Show,* about eight months before the Stones got the nod, the most subversive thing about them is that the grownups were already in on it.

The "sixties," such as they were, had not yet taken hold. The Beatles weren't part of any sort of counterculture, they were part of the establishment—they came *adult-approved.* This wasn't about revolution, this was the wholesale embrace of product.

Keith gives the drums a go, Charlie and Bill have a larf, before taping Thank Your Lucky Stars, *1963.* (Tony Gale, Pictorial Press Ltd./Alamy)

They had already been on television numerous times, and had done their thing shaking their mop-tops and cracking a few jokes for an approving Queen of England at a Royal Command Performance—not an easy gig to get. They were smart, not coming to America until they had a bona fide No. 1 hit. Everything was planned, programmed, and not at all punk—they were cute and loveable, and anyone who didn't get it was just an old square, a hater. But there was no *danger*. Elvis the Pelvis had been in and out of the army and was now busy making increasingly absurd movies, and Little Richard had found God. The first rock'n'roll crisis had faded, and somehow the Negro menace had not taken over America.

Oldsters *hrrummphed* at these Beatles because they had hair that crawled over their collars, but these were the squares and stiffs who'd get hip fast or who'd end up on ice, their relevance having about the same life expectancy as a pig in a slaughterhouse.

The Beatles were actually quite well groomed. Even their bangs were perfect. And when they first appeared on American television, on *The Ed Sullivan Show*, in February of 1964, in front of a roomful of screaming, barely pubescent young women (and seventy-three million viewers at home), the depth of their sexuality, at least publicly, ran to "I Want to Hold Your Hand."

And this always kills me: among the songs they played for Ed Sullivan and America on their big coming out was "Till There Was You," a selection from the popular Broadway musical *The Music Man*—the same hoary piece of shit that gave us cornpone crud like "76 Trombones."

It was not rock.

It was not roll.

It *lilted*, and if you are wondering how this snuck in to the show, or to whom they were pandering, please let me tell you: grownups, that's who, fucking *grownups*. It was a nod and a wink toward safety, and don't let anyone tell you otherwise.

The Beatles were *middlebrow*—meaning, in this case, that anyone could watch them and feel hip—and middle-class approved, which is why so many suddenly inspired young people were able to buy guitars the very next day. Because *their parents approved*, and their parents were the ones with the dough.

The Beatles were the reason a zillion bands got started, from

Black Sabbath to the Ramones—for the love of all that is holy, it seems that everyone who saw that show decided to go out and buy a guitar and form a band THAT VERY SAME DAY.

Girls went nuts for this guitar thing, and guys were nuts for the things girls went nuts for. Those deemed not talented enough to play the guitar were brought to the drum department. Which is one of the sad truths drummers have had to endure: we are treated like the chiropractors of the music industry.

Rock'n'roll is not something I personally ever enjoyed with my family. That just isn't the way the world was supposed to work. Rock'n'roll was supposed to pit teenagers against parents. Rock'n'roll was for libertines, miscreants, and troublemakers. That was the proper order of things.

When the Stones hit *The Ed Sullivan Show*, Mick looked like he had just rolled out of bed and thrown on the first thing he could find,[8] and who knows who or what he left tangled up in his dirty sheets. It was a radical departure from the Beatles, who were so over-groomed they looked as if they were about to be trotted off to the Westminster Dog Show to collect their ribbons. Charlie, of course, ever the snazzy dresser, held the line. He was a man of true style. And he didn't smile too much when he played. The best jazzers never did.

When the Beatles played Chuck Berry, it was adorable, family fun. When the Stones played Chuck, they sounded like they were committing a crime. The Beatles also lacked one other major bit of

8 Obviously his subscription to *DownBeat* had lapsed.

mojo in their live performance: they had no pretty boy handling the mic like a hot cock.

Through a rollicking version of Chuck Berry's "Around and Around," a song about the police breaking up an all-night party, and the honey-tongued, off-speed "Time Is on My Side"—what was known in the trade as a "pussy pleaser"—you could smell the Stones' sex pouring off of the television screen. They sounded *black*, and it did not go unnoticed. There was pandemonium in the studio—screaming girls driving Ed to the brink of insanity—and not a dry seat in the house, but it hardly matched the outrage of the "grownups."

Telegrams and angry phone calls from the pearl-clutchers and guardians of the moral good came flooding in, and as for Ed Sullivan, who had full-throatedly endorsed the Beatles (and eventually Elvis), he declared that "the Rolling Stones will never be back on our show. If things can't be handled, we'll stop the whole business. We won't book any more rock'n'roll groups and will ban teenagers from the theater. ... It took me seventeen years to build this show and I'm not going to have it destroyed in a matter of weeks!"

Apparently, though, the Stones were good for business, and Ed booked them six more times, culminating in 1969, when they capped off their run with "Gimme Shelter," "Love in Vain," and "Honky Tonk Women," and by which time the Beatles had already been off the road for a few years, having completely given up on being a live band. Which is why the Rolling Stones will always be the Beatles' superiors—because they *played*.

∘ ∘ ∘

When Muddy Waters sang "I Just Can't Be Satisfied," the Rolling Stones were listening. Or maybe they picked it up from Chuck Berry, who sang, "*I don't get no satisfaction from the judge*" on his country-blues stomp-rocker "Thirty Days." Who knows, they were certainly intimate with both tunes.

But it wasn't until God came to Keith Richards in a dream—the same God that had delivered symphonies and serenades to Mozart, and funk to James Brown, Mozart and James being self-avowed vessels for His great works—and handed him the riff that became "(I Can't Get No) Satisfaction" that it all began to make sense.

Fortunately for God and teenagers everywhere, Keith was smart enough to wake up and hum the riff into his little portable Philips tape recorder before falling back asleep—the portable tape recorder being quite the happening technology of the time, and a toy that would become a large part of the secret recipe when Keith began abusing it to distort the sound of his acoustic guitar. But more on that later. The song that he laid down that night, half-asleep, *made* the Rolling Stones.

If "Satisfaction" wasn't exactly a textbook example of *anticipation*, then it certainly was one of *frustration*. But by now the Stones knew the score—*satisfaction* isn't what put asses in seats, *not* getting satisfaction was what brought 'em in and left 'em wanting more.

This was the apex of the Stones' first phase. "Satisfaction" made them—No. 1 in the UK! No. 1 in the USA! No. 1 in Italy! In Germany! No. 1 in the World!—and it was likewise some next level shit for Charlie Watts, who doesn't swing "Satisfaction" as much as he drives it through the floor, challenging every accepted notion of how a polite rock'n'roll drummer (never mind a jazz drummer!) was supposed to behave. The studio version of the song was already a bludgeon to the status quo, but unleashed live, it was a full-frontal attack on the modern world, relentless, aggressive, willfully confrontational, the first genuine punk rock song.[9]

---

9 You can slice it as fine as you like, but "Satisfaction" was the beginning. I mean, one could argue that the water had been broken with "Surfin' Bird" by the Trashmen in 1963, a ridiculously outré blast of enthusiasm, subversive in its childish lyrics and unapologetic abuse of reverb and echo, and later embraced by the Cramps and the Ramones, but being adopted by punk-rockers doesn't necessarily make you a punk-rocker, viz. Eddie Cochran, Link Wray, the Troggs, or a raft of other visionary primitives. Bob Dylan was definitely *punk* when he whipped out some of the most aggressive, confrontational, antiestablishment assaults ever perpetrated on a bunch of moldy figs at the 1965 Newport Folk Festival, when he turned up the volume and announced that he was no longer to be found working on Maggie's Farm, but it wasn't *punk rock* any more than indictments like "Subterranean Homesick Blues" or "Positively Fourth Street" were, as incendiary as was the former, or venomous as was the latter. A more pure form of the art began to percolate in 1964 and 1965—the Kinks were positively vicious with "You Really Got Me," but at the end of the day it was still just a song about a chick, no revolution there. The Who were cooking up their first great pop explosion—"My Generation" definitely qualified, but it didn't drop till almost a year later, and the MC5, whose blistering energy would launch a thousand ships, were just getting started, as were the Velvet Underground (who pursued a decidedly darker strain of noise). Better candidates for "the first punk rock band" in those years were the Sonics from Seattle (whose drummer, Bob Bennett, played with the "space-plus beat"), and especially the Monks, whose *avant* hate-rock, and determination to be the most unattractive band extant by shaving bald spots in their heads and dressing like actual medieval monks, put them in a class of their own when they dropped their aural manifesto *Black Monk Time* in 1966 … or Peruvian surf freaks Los Saicos, whose fuzz-ladled 1965 "Demolicion"

The film of their '65 jaunt through Ireland—*Charlie Is My Darling*—is a raw and wonderful document of the band driving crowds to ecstasy with their outlaw formulary of soul, blues, and now "Satisfaction," and, as the title (taken from a popular eighteenth-century Scottish ballad) indicates, a solid first move toward putting Charlie front and center, because, even then, they *knew*.

Before "Satisfaction," Charlie had been steadily evolving—on *Out of Our Heads*, he copped the cool soul strut of Don Covay's "Mercy, Mercy," and the Motown style on Marvin Gaye's "Hitch Hike,"[10] and on *December's Children (And Everybody's)* he amped up

---

is oft-cited by train spotters as a punk rock progenitor (it is about blowing up a train station, after all) ... or any of the hundreds of garage bands that popped up in the wake of Beatlemania, recording high-energy novelty songs that would later provide inspiration for hepcats and proto-punks, especially when they began showing up on compilation records like *Nuggets* and *Back from the Grave*. Which begs the musical question, *If a tree falls in a garage, what sound does it really make?* Inarguably, "Satisfaction" was the first punk-rock song to bust out in to the public consciousness in any meaningful way, and you have to wonder, without "Satisfaction" to guide them, would the MC5 ever have landed on the riff to "Kick Out the Jams"? No matter, I'm taking the Justice Potter approach to punk rock here—I know it when I see it.

10 Marvin, himself an on-and-off Motown house drummer for a few years, played the beat on this one, though it would be criminal not to mention Benny Benjamin, Motown's main man on the drums for many of their earliest hits, and part of the crew that became known as the Funk Brothers. Benjamin, another jazzer turned to R&B, struggled with alcoholism and died far too young, at the age of forty-three, in 1969. Uriel Jones and Richard "Pistol" Allen took over as Benjamin's health failed, but so great was his groove that his influence was felt across their time behind the kit as well—and the influence of the three of them on soul and R&B and the Rolling Stones is practically unimaginable.

the vibe on the hyper-kinetic version of Larry Williams's "She Said Yeah" and the incredibly groovy live version of "Route 66."[11]

But "Satisfaction" was a riff-basher of the highest order, five

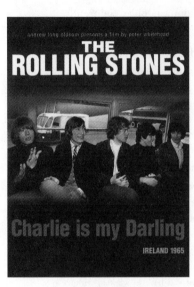

notes—or three, depending on how you're counting—that changed the world. Beethoven did it in four, but that was then, and this was now. "Satisfaction" was transformational. It was transcendent. It certainly wasn't the soul or pure blues that had formed them, although it had something in common with both, which is no doubt why Otis Redding found it so easy to adopt. But in Mick's mouth, and in the hands of the Stones, it was the Big Bang, and Charlie Watts was at the center of the event. Phil Spector called "Satisfaction" not just a song but a "contribution."

They came back quickly with "Get Off of My Cloud"—not in the same league as "Satisfaction," but with a terrific drum hook that was pointing them in the right direction. They still had some of that baroque crud in their systems—I blame the Beatles for pulling them over to the dark side with crap like "As Tears Go By" and "Lady Jane"—but the scorchers were brutal, swung hard, and showed off plenty Charlie's jazz game, especially the psychotic

---

11 Referring to the American releases here, trying not to get lost in the differences between UK and US issues.

reactions of "19th Nervous Breakdown" and "Have you Seen Your Mother, Baby, Standing in the Shadow?"

There were some great bits of drumming on the last couple of records with Brian before things went completely off the rails, particularly on *Between the Buttons*—"My Obsession" and "Complicated" are revered among garage-rockers for their primitive, stomping beats, and the seductive "Miss Amanda Jones" was a harbinger of things to come, with Charlie rolling hard straight into a very aggressive rhythm guitar. With every album, Charlie seemed more in control.

There was now a hot blue bolt of electricity that ran straight from Chico Hamilton to Muddy Waters and Chuck Berry, to a new form of modern rhythm music that was no longer content to swing in the conventional sense. The Rolling Stones were cauterizing the gap between the past and the future, with Charlie Watts providing the beat.

Charlie and Shirley Watts at Brian Jones's funeral, 1969. Bill Wyman was the only other Stone to attend. (PA Images via Getty Images)

FOUR

CHARLIE'S GOOD TONIGHT

IMAGINE YOU HAVE A BROOM. Just a regular old broom. It performs exactly as promised, and fulfills every expectation one might have of a broom.

Now imagine that after a few years of successfully sweeping the kitchen and the garage, the handle breaks. And so you get a new handle, screw it into the broom head, and continue on as if nothing had happened. My question to you is: is it still the same broom?[1]

---

1 The "broom paradox" was famously cast on British sitcom *Only Fools and Horses*, and based on the thought experiment on the metaphysics of identity known as the "Ship of Theseus," popular with Heraclitus and Plato and that lot, and later scribbled down by Plutarch, the gist being that there is a famous ship preserved in a harbor, and as the old planks and parts decayed, they were replaced one by one, until, after a century or so, all of its parts had been replaced. It was a real crowd-splitter, even then.

Don't answer yet. Now imagine that another few years go by, and one day you decide that the head of the broom has had enough. The bristles have gotten soft, and it is no longer doing its job. And so you get a new broom head, and put it on the handle, and continue sweeping. Now, is this still the same broom with which you began this adventure? It performs exactly the same function, fills the exact same space in the household broom landscape, its essence and "broominess" fully intact.

Now imagine that you had put the original broom handle and head in the garage, and they sat on a shelf with a bunch of other junk for a few years, and then in a moment of madness you decide to repair them and put them back together.

You now have two brooms, and the question is: is the reconstructed broom still the original broom, and, if so, then what of the "new" broom? They both have direct roots in the "original" broom, and enough provenance to legitimately claim their identity as "broom."

Or, is it possible that the brooms *don't even exist*, because in this universe, at least, the same object cannot possibly exist in two places?

Now let's imagine the broom is the band Black Sabbath.

Did you know that, since they formed in 1968, Black Sabbath have employed *over twenty-five different members* for various tours and records?

Singer Ozzy Osbourne was the first to go, replaced by a guy named Dave Walker, who had previously been in Savoy Brown and then Fleetwood Mac for a hot second. That didn't stick. Ozzy came back for a flash, and then was replaced by Ronnie James Dio, who would come and go and eventually find great favor with Sabbath fans, even as their sound changed radically without Ozzy's Birmingham twang. Then Geezer Butler split, having been not only their bass player but also their principal lyricist. Then he was back. Then he was out, and their "offstage keyboard player," Geoff Nicholls, played bass for a spell.[2] Deep Purple singer Ian Gillan was in for a record and a tour, and drummer Bill Ward was out again, and Bev Bevan was in—formerly of the Move and a founding member of the Electric Light Orchestra, the kind of organization pooh-poohed by hardcore Sabbath fans, or at least you would think so. Vinnie Appice, of the Appices of Brooklyn, had a go at the drums, before Ward was back, but meanwhile guys with the unlikely names of Ron Keel and David "Donut" Donato sat in for the job originally handled by Ozzy. Then Dave Spitz was in on bass, before Glenn Hughes, who had also sung with Deep Purple, sang for a while, before he was out, and a guy from New Jersey called Ray Gillen was in, and on and on, with another half-dozen or so drummers coming in and out over the years, including the excellent Cozy Powell (ex of the Jeff Beck Group, and Rainbow,

---

2 The offstage keyboard player is a sadly common phenomenon, especially in heavy metal bands who need a synth player to fatten up the sound but believe being seen with keyboards in the band would sully their cock-rock pose, so they are kept hidden behind a curtain or screen, or sequestered under the stage. Aside from Black Sabbath, who used an offstage keyboard player for forty years, KISS, Aerosmith, and Iron Maiden have all depended on them. Even a down-to-earth guy like Bruce Springsteen has succumbed, using Van Halen's offstage guy on his allegedly "solo" performances in 2005.

and who at some point replaced Carl Palmer in Emerson, Lake & Palmer, conveniently becoming the "P" in ELP), and Eric Singer, who later not only joined popular American kabuki band KISS, but also adopted original KISS drummer Peter Criss's signature cat makeup, and assumed Criss's *actual identity*, at least as far as Singer was now *a giant cat playing the drums for KISS*.[3]

The low point of this exercise had to be the lineup of Geoff Nicholls on keys (not hidden behind a screen for a change), Tony Martin on vocals, Bob Daisley on whatever, and former Clash drummer Terry Chimes sitting in for a few moments (Cozy Powell had come and gone a few times by now), with only Tony Iommi offering any legitimate provenance traceable to the original Sabbath lineup, and if you are wondering about the "broominess" of this lineup, you can watch the smelly video they made and judge for yourself, but no one who was a fan of BLACK SABBATH could possibly have mistaken this group for "Black Sabbath," no matter what their label and their lawyers insisted.

o o o

---

3 Which begs yet more existentialism from a place where there really ought not be any. Was he pretending to be the guy in the cat makeup that he had just replaced, *without any concession to the fact that it was now an entirely different cat*, or was he now in fact "The Cat," *as if there were only one Cat*, or *was he just another cat who played the drums, and, if so, were all cats who played the drums interchangeable?* And, if not, did it matter? And, if so, to whom? One thing is for sure, it crapped not only on whatever intelligence quotient may or may not have been credited to KISS fans, but also on the basic concept of identity that most people rely on as a matter of common sense.

After John Bonham died, Led Zeppelin called it quits. Over the years, they've done a few shows with John Bonham's son Jason sitting in, performing a perfectly good-spirited simulacra of the Zeppelin experience, and if it was not entirely the thing itself, it was damn close. But at least one member of the troupe had the horse sense not to carry on with him as "Led Zeppelin," because Led Zeppelin is not a fucking broom.

o o o

To paraphrase Pablo Picasso, drummers are either treated like gods or doormats, and within a very short time after Keith Moon died, he was demoted from former to latter, and replaced in the Who by ex-Faces drummer Kenney Jones.

Putting Kenney Jones in for Moon was like trading Jackson Pollock for a house painter. Perhaps Pete Townshend was looking forward to playing with someone who could keep decent time, or wasn't a complete lunatic, which might have worked for a lot of bands, but not this one.[4] Once Jones was installed, whatever revolution they had once led, it was all over now. And yet no matter how lousy their records were, or how heartbreaking it was to watch Jones try to restore life to the act, they soldiered on, leveraging

---

4 John Entwistle on Keith Moon in *Drum Magazine*: "Keith didn't particularly keep time too well. If he was feeling down the songs would be slow, if he was feeling up the songs would be too fast … I would get very frustrated because he couldn't actually play hi-hat at all, just a mess of cymbals … at times, it could sound like a drum kit falling downstairs. … He tuned all the toms to the same note … when he had the two-deep kit, they'd more or less be tuned to the same note, so if he missed one he'd get the other."

the diminished expectations of classic-rock fans willing to look the other way so that they might go to work the next day having claimed to have seen the Who, until finally announcing that last refuge of a legend, the Farewell Tour.

Good for business, that whole farewell tour thing—even if it turned out not to be the case.

In fact, I believe they invented the farewell tour, and were the first to renege on it. Anyway, they packed Shea Stadium in New York, home of the New York Mets—and briefly home of the Beatles of Liverpool, England—for two successive nights. Even then, box-office bonanza that it was, it must have stung to get outplayed and outclassed by the Clash, whom the Who had personally invited to open up for them, thinking that they were doing the righteous thing by handing them "the torch," as if in 1980 any such torch were the Who's to give.

Eventually they found the right drummer in Zak Starkey. Starkey was Ringo's kid, and he had *provenance*, not to mention the raw talent and Moon-like enthusiasm for hitting everything in sight, but he also understood the *musical* implications of Moon's abstract expressionism without trying to cop it note-for-note, and they managed to put on oddly convincing shows, a lot of which had to do with returning to the original formula of drums and guitar chasing each other, indulging in abandon, and tempos be damned.

The right drummer is hard to find. The kind of competence Kenny Jones offered was worthless in this group. Finding Starkey was one in a million: a cat whose ego was big enough to sit in

Keith Moon's chair and push the drums forward, and challenge the guitarist to keep up with him, but who was humble enough to know what the job was, which was to put the other guys over.

o o o

Here is something else they don't teach you in music theory class:

Duke Ellington was once asked how, after decades of playing, his octogenarian sax-man Johnny Hodges still played so great every night, how he still got that famous liquid tone. How could he possibly muster the enthusiasm and wind to deliver every night, without fail?

"Because he still thinks it will get him laid," was Duke's answer.

I bring this up because sex is the great motivator, and, if you are in a hot band, the odds are that you are going to get some.

At some point, all male hetero-normative rock musicians expect to hook up *just for being in a band*, because they have been told that there will always be some mark who goes for the ol' okeydoke. On a good night, even the bass player has half a chance. The bass player in KISS, a band so ugly that they had to cover their faces with Spackle and grease paint, has claimed more sexual conquests than Wilt Chamberlain and Satan combined.

And so it is not inconsequential that it was around the time when the Stones were just breaking in America that Charlie got married, between tours, tying the knot with Shirley Ann Shepherd, a sculpture student, on October 14, 1964. He was twenty-three years old, and he had met his wife before he met the Stones, and he has been with her ever since, faithfully by all accounts.

Asked how he managed to avoid the trappings of being a rock star, he told the interviewer, simply, "I am not a rock star."

This speaks well to the character of Charlie Watts, I would say.

o o o

Anyone who has ever been in a band knows that there is usually at least one person who isn't really part of the group. He got the gig because he had a station wagon and a PA, or his uncle owned a bar, or he had played drums in the Faces, and it seemed like a good idea at the time.

These are the groups that do not last. There are lots of competent musicians out there, cats who can get through the set with a minimum of discord. There is also a bumper crop of idiots with no taste: talent-show singers high on their own melisma; drummers who can't help but hit that cymbal on the Cole Porter song; bass players who are confused because their guitars only have four strings.

Great bands are *gangs*. They stick together. This doesn't mean that they have to love each other, or even like each other that much—anyone who has hung out with bands who have been together for any length of time knows the kind of kvetching and bickering and bullshit that goes on—but once you've vanquished the weak link, and manifested the elusive group of people who can vibrate around a common core, and the sum has become far greater than the parts, that is something you really do not want to fuck with.

"Charlie coolly positions himself somewhere in the middle," Bill observes in his memoir, *Stone Alone*. "He was able to be mates with everybody, flit from one another and communicate with all of us quite naturally. Charlie's easygoing character is his strength. … What endeared Charlie to everyone was his imperturbable, laid-back, no pop-star, friendly approach … many people observe that on stage he seems detached from us, that because music is a form of religion to him and he is totally immersed in it. We are lucky to have him, for the drums are the foundation of our sound."

"Everybody thinks Mick and Keith are the Rolling Stones," Keith told *Rolling Stone*. "If Charlie wasn't doing what he's doing on drums, that wouldn't be true at all. You'd find out that Charlie Watts is the Stones."

The idea to put Charlie Watts on the cover of *Get Yer Ya-Ya's Out*, the live document of the Rolling Stones' 1969 American tour—the year they truly became THE GREATEST ROCK'N'ROLL BAND IN THE WORLD—was far more than a bit of comic anti–front man irony (Mick wasn't much for irony, anyway), it was a sure sign of how Charlie was regarded in the band. Mick even let him borrow his hat for the photo, the red, white, and blue top hat of which he was quite fond. And if that weren't enough fluffing by Mick, his famous between-song exaltation—"Charlie's good tonight, ain't he?"—put the drummer over. The only other person to get a shout-out on that record was Mick's trousers, who lost a button and were at risk of falling down.

∘ ∘ ∘

Mick's trousers were hardly the biggest problem that year. This is the tour that saw Meredith Hunter die at the Altamont speedway at

Keeping an eye on Mick's trousers. Live in 1969, from the film Gimme Shelter. *(Photofest)*

the final show of the tour, dead at the hands of the Hells Angels hired to do security for this shambolic free concert, captured on the film *Gimme Shelter*, and universally decried as the death of the hippie dream.

They had come a long way since their last American tour in 1966, which was still fueled by the vapors of Beatlemania, when they were the scruffy bad boys of the British Invasion beat bands, playing to screaming audiences not yet old enough to drink.

A lot had happened between 1966 and 1969, not least of all crossing the Rubicon of LSD. The Stones had turned from black-and-white to color, as had their audience. Virginal teeny boppers had given way to veterans of the Summer of Love: stoners, burnouts, freaks, draft dodgers, and part-time revolutionaries, not to mention fashion models, intellectuals, film directors, artists, and the rest of drug-culture aristocracy.

They were living in a highly accelerated culture—the miniskirt had been invented, and men were on their way to the moon. It should have been an optimistic time, but a lazily constructed highlights reel of the day would not have been complete without a double dose of murder and assassination (now recurring themes in the Rolling Stones' work), anti-war protesters being clubbed by cops in riot gear at the Chicago Democratic convention, the Paris uprisings, the carpet-bombing of Vietnam, and Richard Nixon flashing a "V for Victory" sign. This is all highly reductive, of course, but you get the idea—the hangover of 1968 can still be heard on any classic-rock radio station, or in any baby boomer's record collection. Paul McCartney sang "Helter Skelter" on the Beatles' "White Album," the loudest, most abrasive moment of his career, inadvertently inspiring a string of murders in the Hollywood Hills, and the Rolling Stones delivered "Sympathy for the Devil," in which Mick solves the mystery of the Kennedy assassination, not to mention "Street Fighting Man," which vented the frustrations of would-be rebels caught in a world of compromise solutions.

Before the Rolling Stones became THE GREATEST ROCK'N'ROLL BAND IN THE WORLD, they had to get back to where they began: *maracas, tremolo-thick guitars, gospel shouting, violent harmonicas …* this is what they were about. Bo and Little Richard, Chuck and Muddy. Except now it was time to take it all into a brave new world. No more simple declarations of "how it's gonna be," the time was right for a palace revolution. Among other things, it would cost them a guitar player.

o o o

This fresh brace of revolutionary fervor came on the heels of the Stones' first great misstep—*Their Satanic Majesties Request*.

Misstep because, count on it, with the single exception of swinging back against pesky punk-rockers and giving their guitar rock a fair shake on the discotheque floor, every attempt by the Rolling Stones to chase a trend has been an abject failure. From falling under the sway of the Beatles and trying to spin baroque pop hits out of recorders and Mellotrons, and then trying to create their own *Sgt. Pepper's*, flashing forward a few decades to Mick hiring hip-hop producers to keep up with the times, every time they lurched away from the truth that was the Rolling Stones, the results were at best forgettable, at worst the kind of thing you might forgive but never forget.[5]

In sober reality, *Satanic* wasn't as bad as its reputation, just a sort of a lackluster dalliance in lysergic purgatory, the path one had to travel to get to the next destination: in this case, their first masterpiece, *Beggars Banquet*.

---

5 John Lennon to *Rolling Stone*, 1971: "I'd just like to list that what we did and what the Stones did two months after on every fucking album. Every fucking thing we did, Mick does exactly the same. He imitates us. And I would like one of you fucking underground people to point it out: *Satanic Majesties Request* is *Pepper*. 'We Love You' is the most fucking bullshit, that's 'All You Need Is Love.' I resent the implication that the Stones are revolutionaries and the Beatles weren't."

But before there was *Beggars Banquet*, there was "Jumpin' Jack Flash," recorded just as they were getting ready to work on the new long-player, and released as a single in 1968. "Jumpin' Jack Flash" was to hard rock what "Satisfaction" was to punk.

"I can hear the whole band take off behind me every time I play 'Flash,'" Keith remarks in his book. "There's this extra sort of turbo overdrive. You jump on the riff, and it plays *you*. We have ignition? OK, let's go."

"It was trying to get past the acid," Mick would later comment, and indeed, they had punched through the wall and come out the other side changed, and better for it.

Charlie largely abstained from drugs, which matters not because being straight in this group of hooligans speaks to any higher power or moral authority (let's not forget, Charlie was a bebop freak and well-acquainted with the jazz cigarettes that were the coin of the realm, and was never afraid to take a sip), but because while everyone else was in orbit around him getting into an increasingly heavy drug scene, he held the center, and gave the song a perfect ride without any frippery or flourish.

His part on "Jumpin' Jack Flash" is as minimal as anything he's ever cut. Simply, he let the singer and the guitar player do the heavy lifting (Keith also lends a hand, beating up on a floor tom to give it that adult dose of *thwack* and *thump*), and doesn't even move from the hi-hat to the ride cymbal on the chorus, a cheap-but-effective move that has become pretty much standard play in any rock song, nor does he indulge in any unfortunate accents on the crash cymbals.

"Jumpin' Jack Flash" was the first thing the Stones cut with their new producer, Jimmy Miller, whose most recent résumé included a pair of successful records by Traffic, and whose rhythmic sense and simpatico were perfect for a group that needed some direction, but not too much. Miller was a vibe master, a groove guy, and knew how to work between the group and the engineer to get the sounds and the songs. He created *flow*.

"He wasn't a great drummer," Charlie says of Miller in the Stones' own oral history, "but he was great at playing drums on records, which is a completely different thing … Jimmy actually made me stop and think about the way I played the drums in the studio, and I became a much better drummer in the studio thanks to him—together we made some of the best records we've ever made. … One-sixth of those songs was Jimmy, for me. Mick might say, 'That's rubbish, you did it all yourself,' but that's the way I feel. Jimmy taught me how to discipline myself in the studio."

As it is, a hundred other drummers would have ruined "Jumpin' Jack Flash," looking for places to push their way in. Charlie, with Miller standing behind him, drove straight down the middle of the road, and it was flawless. And credit must be given to Mick on the maracas—they learned well from Bo Diddley (and Jimmy Miller)—whipping out the shakers was like pouring gasoline on a fire. They'd pull them out again when they needed the extra *zork*: listen for the maracas to combust right after the sax solo in "Brown Sugar," they come in *extremely* loud, just before the fader gets pulled back into the relative-safety zone; and after the second chorus in "Gimme Shelter," anticipating the harmonica entrance and the guitar solo, not to mention the wailing of rape and murder. On "Street Fighting Man," upon Mick's final command to "Get down!" the maracas explode like a Molotov cocktail hitting the front door of a bank. Suddenly the revolution had begun. It was an insurrection in simplicity, especially at a time when rock'n'roll was getting bigger, louder, dumber, and whiter, and the idea of maracas likely seemed quaint to the uninitiated.

∘ ∘ ∘

There were some terrific drummers coming out of the era, men who powered their bands through brute force and extended technique. There were also lot of charlatans and show-offs, wannabe Bonhams and Bakers, guys who couldn't do more than keep time but somehow found themselves banging it out with the band of local stoners, Cinderella dreaming at a time when hard rock was becoming an adolescent fetish.

By 1970, Black Sabbath and Led Zeppelin had released their first records, and the heavy style was now officially a thing. The irony is that the heaviest cats coming up in those years—Bill Ward in Sabbath and John Bonham in Zeppelin—had the jazz cooked into their veins. Bill Ward's drumming in Sabbath was chock full of Krupa-isms and Louie Bellson–like fills, pushing the flash of the big bands into the darkness on songs like "The Wizard" and "Electric Funeral." John Bonham, too, had absorbed Krupa and Max Roach into his style, but mostly it came out when it was time for the big drum solo. He was a master of the shuffle, of *rubato*, misdirection, release, and attack, and had invented a style that seemed at times like a mutation of James Brown's great drummers, Clyde Stubblefield and Jabo Starks, masters of backbeat slight of hand, and Zigaboo Modeliste of the Meters from New Orleans, whose ability to move the beat within the groove was as dizzying as Bonham's would become.

But Bonham was distinctly his own man—one of the few cats, like Charlie Watts and Keith Moon, whose personal vision for rock'n'roll drums was completely unprecedented. Bonham's greatest advancements lay in his monstrous bass-drum technique, perpetrating his famous double strokes and triplets, and balancing an incredible sense of open space against a barrage of untouchable chops.

One of the great things about Led Zeppelin is that like Charlie Watts, Bonham never sounded hurried, even when they were rocking at their hardest. He had great taste and discipline, and even when he was blasting at full strength, he was extremely *musical*. His playing could be rhythmically complex, but it was built from the ground up, not the top down. It was the sort of lesson that was lost on a lot of young drummers who thought they could learn to play the blues by listening to Cream and stomping all over everything.

Keith Moon, another Krupa disciple, *dabbled* in anticipation but couldn't commit—I posit the intro to "I Can See for Miles" as a lovely bit of foreplay—but ultimately Keith wasn't really one for great self-restraint. When it came to the line about getting a "kick out of you" in the Cole Porter song, he would not have been content to hit a crash cymbal, he would have destroyed the entire kit.

Just as the Stones were stripping it down to the bare, knife-edge essentials of druggy country-rock and brooding apocalyptic blues, the Who had become full-tilt art-school maximalists perpetrating grand rock operas, and Moon's drum set had grown like some sort of percussive kudzu, flourishing with drums in every direction. His playing was spectacular, of course, and an extension of his personality—outrageous, wanton, drunk, charismatic, generous, honest, and out of control—but the harm he did to future drummers who could never learn to calm the fuck down and play the song was now planted, and within a few years all the kids who had bought their drums to be like Ringo would be adding a zillion tom-toms and gongs and whoozits to their kits, and measuring their success not in their ability to swing but in new dimensions of excess.

And, as such, a new breed of drummer rose up like a virus in the 1970s: teenaged boys who could fire off a fusillade of triple-flamadiddles across their bank of rapid-tuning Remo Rototoms, but who couldn't play a simple shuffle or a convincing punk-rock beat without getting in the way of themselves. Which begs the question, if you need that much gear, what are you *really* compensating for?

o o o

The Stones' new record, *Beggars Banquet* (1968), wasn't so much a "return to their blues roots," as has been written so often by music writers with no imagination, yobbos who can only see "the blues" as a thing of the past. In reality, *Beggars Banquet* was more of a wild leap into the Stones' future. And, anyway, it was far more country than blues, and more about possibilities than anything else. It was not the sound of a band returning to their previous success, but rather of breaking free from it.

It was also the end for Brian Jones, and if anyone had thought that the Stones couldn't be the Stones without Brian, they would have been wrong. Certainly they could not have *become* the Rolling Stones without Brian, but at some point he had become a spanner in the works—the acid, the lifestyle, and the damaged double helix of psychedelic pop star and bluesman had become too twisted to be viable—and he had to leave. As it was, he wasn't showing up for work anyway. He played bits and pieces here and there, including a lovely bit of slide guitar on "No Expectations," his last thoughtful contribution. Burning out on drugs and pop stardom may well be a cliché, but Brian deserves a lot of credit for making it so.

Some parts can be replaced without making a difference, and yet sometimes the broom gets even better. The Stones hired a new guitarist: a prodigy named Mick Taylor, a veteran of John Mayall's Bluesbreakers, where he had replaced Peter Green, who had fucked off to be in Fleetwood Mac, who had replaced Eric Clapton, who had done same for the promised land of Cream. At some point, the British blues scene felt a lot like one gigantic housewares store.

There was never a more exciting time to be a Rolling Stone. Taylor made it on to a few songs on the next Jimmy Miller–produced Stones record, *Let It Bleed* (1969), and *L'âge d'or Rolling Stones* had officially dawned.

The new band was a decidedly darker, sexier, and more powerful version of the Rolling Stones. Taylor was a viciously capable lead-guitar player with a searing sound, and he put Keith's syncopated rhythm and groove-intense minimalism in sharp relief. The Ancient Art of Weaving—the blurring of guitars that had been achieved with Brian—was out, in favor of a more traditional rhythm/lead relationship, and everyone rose to the challenge. It opened up the sound and made everything cut harder: the songs found new space to breathe, the jams became expansive without losing their edge.

And so Charlie weaved and dodged in between Keith Richards and Bill Wyman, and he put the spotlight on Mick, making sure that every word had the full weight of the groove behind it.

Not content just to *take* drugs, they began to sing about them. Violence, sex, and Satan were the other favored leitmotifs. And as much as it took a great singer like Jagger to deliver the goods, now more than ever he needed the simpatico of the guitar players and the smarts and jazz sensibilities of a thoughtful drummer who understood how to accompany a singer to drive it all home.

Charlie slammed when it was called for, and laid out when the song didn't want drums—he was a humble guy, after all, always putting himself behind the song. But he swung hard, and he punched like a heavyweight when Mick needed him to deliver the knockout blow.[6]

o o o

"Street Fighting Man" on *Beggars Banquet* had opened the door for the Rolling Stones' own heavy style, a wash of guitars and slamming drums, but in fact, the song was largely played on an acoustic

---

6 Later in our story, Charlie will actually punch Mick. The story has been told plenty of times, but everyone always forgets the real ending. Wait for it.

guitar, and Charlie's part was originally performed on something of a toy drum set, a 1930s contraption called the London Jazz Kit, which he had picked up in an antique shoppe. It wasn't much more than some drum heads held together with wire, and folded into a suitcase so that jazz drummers might travel to a gig by train, or bring it along to wreck a party. Charlie used to drag it along on tour so he could unpack it in a hotel room and jam with Keith, and they'd sometimes record themselves on Keith's magic Philips tape recorder, which distorted the living bejeezus out of anything. This is what they brought to the recording studio to lay the foundation for the revolution.

New drums and guitars were overdubbed on top of the cassette recording, and the results were bestial, what Keith would later call Charlie's most important drum part. It was *orchestral*, like a Phil Spector wet dream, scored for countless acoustic guitars and percussion instruments, including an extra, overdubbed bass drum, more cymbals (and of course the maracas), a somewhat impressionistic piano, several tracks of vocals, plus a small raft of psychedelic exotica, including glimmers of strategically placed feedback, tamboura, sitar, and shehnai, the latter being something like an Indian oboe, a double-reed horn heard droning on the outro. The only electric instrument on the track was the bass, played here by Keith, an increasingly common occurrence. At some point, it ceased to even be a *song*—it was more like a manufactured sonic event *based on a song*.

"Gimme Shelter," on *Let It Bleed*, was even more violent and foreboding. They painted the hard rock they had invented black with unhinged gospel and soul, thanks to the hair-raising, gorgeous wail of Merry Clayton, who, not incidentally, had made her bones singing in Ray Charles's band. Mick's over-modulated blues harp took over where Little Walter had left off, and a wicked-cool güiro riff, courtesy of Jimmy Miller, gave the whole melee a dangerously sexy flavor. Charlie's snare, bass drum, and cymbal combinations on the turnarounds were as threatening as anything he had ever played.

Maracas, tremolo-thick guitars, gospel singing, violent harmonicas . . . that shit was always there, and now, in the hands of these newly enlightened Rolling Stones, it seemed to have been broadcast from the future rather than born of some distant past. There was no precedent for this sort of thing: once upon a time, the Stones were just a bunch of beatniks and art students credibly playing black music; now they were agents of chaos playing ROLLING STONES music. There was no difference between black and white, between gospel and hard rock, between Bo Diddley and the apocalypse.

Another thing: somewhere along the way, the Stones had also become a crack country outfit, so good that ten years hence even their punk rock and disco records brought some serious twang. Blues, country, gospel, hard rock, pop, whatever, don't let anyone fool you, it is all the same shit. Charlie Watts and the Rolling Stones figured that out before anyone else of their era—Bob Dylan and the Band, maybe Van Morrison, were on the same track, but with hardly the same vengeance or erotic fixations. Which is just one more reason why the Stones matter. Theirs was a fountain filled with blood.

"Let It Bleed," their second great country number (from the album of the same name), is one of those songs that bar bands almost always ruin, not because it's so hard to play but because, like so many great Stones songs, it lives very specifically in its own tempo—heat it up too much and it sounds like a tawdry rock song, too slow and it drags like creeping death. On top of that, it is a desperate and sleazy song, and requires the precise amount of friction to achieve climax—no more, and hopefully no less.

I remember playing it on one of those gigs I used to let myself get talked into because I was bored, or needed the money, or thought there might be some girls at the gig, and as much as I tried to breathe some spirit into it—I was playing keys at the time[7]— the guys in the band were determined to just *rock out*, because they were stupid and couldn't help themselves, and had obviously spent too much time listening to some aberrational alt-rock crud that had cut the blues and swing and dirt from the plot, when they should have been listening to T. Rex or the Stooges or Hank Williams or some goddam thing that had a direct connection to honest rock'n'roll. They took the Stones for granted as something that was easy to play, and when it came to "Let It Bleed," not only had they never been knifed in a "dirty filthy basement," as the song goes—*which is OK, because, really, who has?*—but they didn't see the romance in it either, which was a problem.

Finally, after holding the line on the tempo, and encouraging a more circumspect approach to the song rather than just using it

---

7 This is what happens to drummers in New York City, among the least kind places for drummers in the world, where everyone's floor is someone else's ceiling, and no one has a garage or basement—we find ourselves playing more apartment-friendly instruments, like keyboards and guitars.

as a mindless vehicle for the guitar player to show off his meager bottleneck skills, I blurted, "IT'S SUPPOSED TO BE *SLEAZY*, IT'S *A DRUGGY COUNTRY SONG, FER CHRISSKAKES*," to which the drummer sniffed "*WE* ARE NOT SLEAZY," and then continued to screw the song like a man just released from a long prison stretch, to which I responded, "NEITHER IS CHARLIE MUTHERFUCKING WATTS, AND IT NEVER STOPPED HIM FROM PLAYING IT RIGHT."

Not that it was ever going to sound like the Rolling Stones, but there is something to be said for good bar bands.

o o o

"Honky Tonk Women," the Stones' first great country song, is another one that the punters never get. Recorded sometime during the *Let It Bleed* sessions (with Jimmy Miller providing the iconic, *slightly* fucked-up cowbell part) and released as a single in the summer of '69, it was the recorded debut of Keith's open-G tuning, and his new approach to rhythm playing. Of course, playing the song right is all about the intro, the nuance of the cowbell, and the little drum spray at the beginning of the song, off the beat—a classic bit of Charlie, an unbalanced fill that a child should be able to play. Unfortunately, there never seem to be any children around when you really need them.

Then again, the Stones never played it quite like that ever again. It was Keith's riff—he owned it, and generally kicked off every live version by striking the open strings on his guitar like a cock-rockin', countrified Svengali, and taking his sweet fucking time with it, too. It was as much attitude as it was music, a riff so simple that it hardly qualified—it's just one chord, and no tricks!—and yet Keith made it so perfectly identifiable, unlike any other G

'GET YER YA-YA'S OUT!'
The Rolling Stones in concert

chord ever hit, dirty and majestic, a call to the dance floor, a tone poem about liquor and drunken sex, written with a Telecaster.

Keith's open-G guitar tuning was the same tuning a lot of Mississippi cats had come up playing in the Delta, but there was no way they could have seen what Keith had in store for this ancient technique, losing the heavy bottom string and turning his six-string electric guitar into a five-string riff machine capable of deforesting continents.

"It's what you leave out that counts," Keith explains in his book. "Five strings cleared out the clutter, it gave me the licks and laid on the textures ... with five strings you can be sparse; that's your frame, that's what you work on. 'Start Me Up,' 'Can't You Hear Me Knockin',' 'Honky Tonk Women' all leave those gaps between chords."

The lessons learned across *Beggars* and *Let It Bleed* were in full force when the Stones took it on the road, and evidenced seductively in the slinky, promiscuous crawl of "Stray Cat Blues," and the blistering version of "Little Queenie," the first time that one of their Chuck Berry covers smoked the original. Keith was no longer just playing Chuck Berry riffs, he was incinerating them.

Get Yer Ya-Ya's Out wasn't just a souvenir from the tour, it was an invitation by the Rolling Stones to get on board or get run over.[8]

Charlie was finding the jazz within, the Keith and Charlie one-two becoming a deadly combination. This was the rock upon which they built their church.

Mick was learning to vamp and spit, and whatever musical innocence they had once been blessed with was now gone. Bill Wyman was flawless in the bass clef—rumbling, walking, driving, fearless, often complex, but never in front, always on top—and Mick Taylor flashed lights in everyone's eyes, cutting through the melee with blinding technique. Even simple songs were becoming soul manifestos. The Rolling Stones had become THE ROLLING STONES. No longer pop stars but ROCK STARS.

As always, Charlie had the best seat in the house, but he was not simply a witness, he was a *participant*. He was an adept who held secret knowledge. He had grown from beat-keeper to shaman. His ghost notes were bubbling like never before, rollin' and tumblin' through the turnarounds—but never did he lay off the backbeat or neglect the kick drum, he knew ancient secrets of how to make a roadhouse dance. It was his picture on the cover of the record, and for good reason: he was the source of the Stones' superpowers. After all, no one dances to the words. No one dances to the guitar solos.

---

8 Worth noting that, like a great majority of so-called live records, *Ya-Ya's* is heavily polished, overdubbed with half a dozen lead vocals and a couple songs worth of guitars, including "Little Queenie." At some point you just have to accept that you really have no idea what you are actually hearing.

FIVE

RIP THIS JOINT

BACK IN THE EARLY DAYS OF ROCK'N'ROLL, when the stiffs and squares were ringing the church bells as warning, terrified of the jungle beat that seemed to inflame the genitalia of their children and threaten the moral fiber of the nation, they were right to be scared, of course.

But they had no clue just how right they were. How were they to see "Brown Sugar" coming? A song about slave girls and dope and cunnilingus and rape and God knows what else, with a riff and a beat and a wailing sax solo from Bobby Keys that added up to less of a pop song than it did a hanging crime. Playing on America's storied past, as it did, naturally it shot to the top of the charts.

Maybe it was the times they lived in, maybe it was the drugs, but at some point, the Stones basically lost any sense of decency, even as they were ascending to become THE GREATEST ROCK'N'ROLL BAND IN THE WORLD.

Beggars Banquet and *Let It Bleed* were besot with sex and drugs and violence, but even they couldn't begin to predict "Brown Sugar," the first single from *Sticky Fingers* (1971), whose B-side (just in case anyone was still hazy on the Rolling Stones' worldview) was something called "Bitch," another song about drugs and liquor and the dark side of love. It was the kind of one-two punch that toppled lesser civilizations.

Not incidentally, before they landed that knockout combination, they had delivered the final single they owed to their record company, a brilliant confection best known as "Cocksucker Blues" (aka "Schoolboy Blues" in polite circles) in which Mick Jagger proves not only his bona fides as a first-rate bluesman, but his absolute willingness to go the distance and take one for the team.

The single was never officially released, but some promos were cut and it was bootlegged in short order, and I don't know any serious Stones fan who doesn't know the words by heart. *Cocksucker Blues* also became the title of a documentary film of the Stones 1972 American tour, directed by photographer Robert Frank—he had done much of the photography for the cover of *Exile on Main St.*—and was instantly notorious for its depiction of roadie antics, band members doing drugs, groupie hijinks, etc., etc., and was quickly denounced by the band and largely banned from being shown, although a decent bootleg is only as far away as the closest internet connection. Mostly it is better left to the imagination.

The musical sections are invigorating—a reminder that in 1972, the Rolling Stones were playing at an altitude that would never again be achieved by *anyone*—but a groupie being passed around on the Stones' plane with Mick and Keith as part of the cheerleading squad, not so much. (Charlie Watts, bless him, walks away, plainly disgusted. The woman's joy in the moment is ambiguous at best.) The final results are an odd *cinema verité* document that probably should never have been made, but is now part of the permanent record: darkly voyeuristic, often tedious, exciting in the way that contraband always is, but depressing in the knowing that the value lies in the cheap thrill of trespassing, not in the thing itself, unless you get off seeing Keith nodding out backstage, a groupie getting a fix, or Mick Taylor smoking pot with a naked woman—the most shocking part of which is that they have no rolling papers and have to build a joint by reconstructing a regular old cigarette, which seems hardly professional for this group of delinquents.

The highlight is Stevie Wonder, the opening act on much of the tour, jamming with the Stones on an encore medley of "Uptight (Everything's Alright)" and "Satisfaction"—which share the same stomping beat—but the candle isn't worth the game. Chalk it up as a failed experiment, or a momentary lapse of judgment—not the first or last time the Stones would be guilty of either, just the most extreme.

o o o

If Charlie Watts didn't exist, the Stones would have had to invent him.

Keith's new style was reaching critical mass. The easygoing open-G chord that opened "Honky Tonk Women" had grown into a beast that needed to be fed—a slashing, chopping riff that was the antithesis to hippie strumming. There was a raw sexuality about his syncopation, there was nothing folksy about it. He played off the beat, usually ahead of it, setting the pace like a warlord and demanding that this mob of Rolling Stones follow him, chains and switchblades at the ready. Which isn't to say that this line of attack couldn't be performed at slower tempos. In fact, when they laid back, it was every bit as insidious and sexual and threatening as it was when they opened up the throttle and let 'er rip.

Theirs was a swing all their own, and they owed its heart, if not its beating soul, to Charlie, who, much like Muhammad Ali, floated like a butterfly and stung like a King Bee.

His right hand was nimble, his cymbal patterns swung like the great heroes of blues and jazz, and his left hand landed just slightly, almost imperceptibly, behind the beat, and when they were hitting their stride the effect was the kind of thing that not only encouraged deviant behavior but seemed like a license for it.

"Something happens when we play together," Bill Wyman explains in his book. "It's impossible to copy. Every band follows the drummer. We don't follow Charlie. Charlie follows Keith. So the drums are very slightly behind Keith. It's only fractional. Seconds. Minuscule. And I tend to play ahead. It's got a sort of wobble. It's dangerous because it can fall apart at any minute."[1]

And therein was the beauty of the thing, the essence of the Stones style—*tight but loose*. It was terribly sexual, and wonderfully

---

1 I think it was Ornette Coleman who said that if the band plays along to the drummer, then it is *rock'n'roll*, and if the drummer plays along to the band, then it is *jazz*.

steamy. It was fluid, viscous, and soaked in sin. Libidinous and licentious. The lessons taught by Chuck Berry and Bo Diddley and James Brown and Little Richard had all sunk into Keith's brain, and this is what came out.

Keith was now *improvising* rhythms, letting his body lead him, grooving from the waist down, *making it up as he went along*, which is the very definition of *jazz*.

There are those who would snort if you told them that Keith was playing *jazz*, but Charlie wouldn't, and that is one more reason Why Charlie Watts Matters, because jazzbo that he was, Charlie was no snob, and he was settling into his own new thing as well, to boldly go where no drummer had gone before.

Pound for pound, Charlie was the hardest-swinging drummer in the rock'n'roll world. Unlike many drummers with more *proper* technique—Charlie's right hand was naturally stronger than his left—he understood that charming inconsistencies and unpredictability were the very essence of style, and he turned his own shortcomings into one of his greatest attributes. You couldn't invent this shit, it was just the way he played naturally.

Charlie's oddball intros and fills built of broken rolls and ruffs were as individual to his style as the color blue was to Marc Chagall, and he had begun using the hi-hat in the most unexpected ways, waging counterintuitive cat-and-mouse battles between snare and hi-hat, opening and closing them in the middle of fills and on the in-between bits, finding jazz in even the simplest of songs. Onstage, it crept into the most unexpected places, from the once fundamental drum part of "Jumpin' Jack Flash"—which was now filigreed with explosive accents, machine-gun snare rolls, and inside-out hi-hat magic—to the country numbers "Let It Bleed" and "Dead Flowers," whose earthy chord changes blossomed into explosions of color. The intro to "All Down the Line," already a balletic bit of drum banter, would explode over the years into an expressionist masterpiece.

The famous lifting of the stick—hitting the snare drum without hitting the hi-hat on the two and four, a simple technique that gave the snare hits a little more presence—would mostly come later, and further solidify the Charlie Watts style. It's one of those things that drummers talk about when they talk about Charlie, because it is one of the very few things about him that is easy to describe. Charlie has always said he didn't even realize he was doing it until it was pointed out to him, and then he wrote it off as being lazy, even as it helped define his style.

He had already mastered artful tics like using the ride cymbal judiciously, instead of the crash cymbal, as an accent, a highlight, a little pepper in the sauce, avoiding the usual overpowering *kaboom*, the kind of big rock cymbal thing that John Bonham loved to lean on.[2] Later, Charlie began using the crash cymbals to ride on, coloring the sound as a jazz player would, and even through the din of the Stones playing live, it added just the right note, a sublime shift, because songs are not just verses and choruses and middle-eights and intros and solos and whatnot—that's too easy, too modular. Charlie was a jazz cat who knew there were no rules about coloring

2 And again, this is why when you are listening to Led Zeppelin when you are stoned you think you hear the phone ringing when really it's not.

outside the lines. You blended colors when you needed to.

When Brian was in the band, Charlie played the *drums*. Now, more and more, it seemed like he was playing the *band*.

o o o

Much has been written about *Exile on Main St.*, its creation a towering part of the Stones' mythology. And, once again, it is hard to imagine anyone coming in completely naked, but here's the gist: the Stones, on self-imposed tax exile in France, go looking for a place to record. Unable to find a suitable studio, they decamp at Keith's house, *Nellcôte*, a Côte d'Azur mansion that was once a Gestapo outpost of some sort, with swastikas still on the drain gates in the basement. And this is where they set up to make the greatest rock'n'roll record of all time, to be recorded on the Rolling Stones Mobile Studio, which will eventually become a legend in its own right, going on to be used by the Who, Fleetwood Mac, and Bob Marley, to name just a few. Led Zeppelin, who didn't have a basement per se, but had something called a Headley Grange, also used it to great success.

Much of *Exile* was recorded at night, the schedule largely being written around the drug habits of Keith Richards.[3] The band would descend to the basement after dark, with a galaxy of girlfriends and drug dealers and hangers on burning the midnight

3 Of course, the less romantic part of the story is how much of the Stones' basement tapes were overdubbed, sweetened, fixed, polished, and otherwise completed in the somewhat less mythologized confines of Sunset Sound in Los Angeles. But you sure as hell can hear the drugs and basement sweat all over the damn thing.

Mick, Charlie, and Mick, living on Keith
time: Inglewood Forum, Los Angeles, 1972.
(Ethan Russell © Ethan Russell)

oil and every other goddam thing upstairs. Everyone who didn't have a junk problem, it would seem, left with one, or would be well on their way.

Charlie and Bill lived safely down the road apiece, and, as Keith followed his muse, weren't always around when Keith was ready to record.

Jimmy Miller was beginning to flag—how anyone could herd these cats let alone keep up with Keith without dying was itself a minor miracle—but he managed, along with engineer Glyn Johns, to keep things moving, even as he began to adopt Keith's worst habits, and he even played the drums on a few tracks including "Shine a Light," "Happy" (mostly because Charlie wasn't around, hedging his bets like the rest of them on whether they'd find Keith vertical, horizontal, or in some horrible state in between), and a bit of "Tumbling Dice," which is another story.[4]

A jazz cat named Bill Plummer was hired to play stand-up bass

---

4 Miller had already famously sat in for Charlie on "You Can't Always Get What You Want"—when Charlie was having trouble "finding the groove" that Miller was after, the producer sat down and had at it himself. One might think that Charlie had just gotten bored waiting for the French horn and the choir to finish up their interminable twaddle—another questionable Beatles boost—but of course that was recorded at a later date, such is the magic of modern recording, and therefore not a viable excuse. Miller's groove *is* tricky—skipping the four on the snare during the verses gave the body of the song a looser feel and created a greater sense of release at the end of the song, not to mention that it also insured that no bar band would ever get it right. Charlie wasn't thrilled with Miller sitting down at the drums, but by all accounts he was graceful about it. In later live versions, Charlie invariably hit the backbeat on the two *and* four, which made it possibly less funky than the record, but the lesson here is that you can't always get what you want, not when you are playing in twenty-thousand-seat sheds: the studio and the stage are different things, the first being about creating a space that may not even exist, the latter about moving air. Anyway, the real hook to the song wasn't the beat, it was bonkers turnarounds, *played aggressively but melodically* on the drums—*"If you try some time, you just might find, you get what you need"*—filling the air with shrapnel and putting the blissful gospel of the verses and the religious urgency of the choruses into sharp contrast. This was all Charlie, and this is where the song lived. On "Tumbling Dice," Miller comes in just at the end, another example of it being easier to sit down and play the damn thing rather than spend the afternoon trying to explain it, and with a pair of scissors and some Scotch tape (because that's how records used to be made), *voila.* More importantly, "Tumbling Dice" is a legendary example of a song that lives in its own *very specific* tempo—it allegedly took over 150 takes for Keith to find the exact sweet spot, and it remained a sore point for years with Mick, who always wanted to pick it up a bit when they played it live. Judging by the recorded documents, Mick always won those battles—after all, you make records in poetry but play the gig in prose—but there is no beating the unhurried swagger of the original.

on a few numbers, and ably pitched in, but, such was the vibe of the Stones that the basement was like a black hole of Rolling Stonesisms, and nothing escaped—no light, no stray riffs—and no matter who played on what, it was Keith's thing, and it never sounded like anything but THE ROLLING STONES.

"All Down the Line" is probably the perfect Stones song. From the jabs of the opening guitar riff and the behind-the-beat Charlie rope-a-dope that fuels it, it's a flawless bit of sparring—soulful, sweet, and sleazy. Even the throwaways on *Exile* shine—"I Just Want to See His Face," "Stop Breaking Down," "Shake Your Hips"—all as necessary a part of the firmament of *Exile* as the stars in the sky.

With Brian Jones, the Stones played *songs*. Now, they played *music*—they had become very capable of stretching out and playing far beyond the Chicago-style blues that sparked their genesis.

Mick was not only a genius at slurring lyrics—he could make anything sound filthy—but also at being a vocal pugilist himself when it came to singing rhythmically, powerfully, unambiguously joyously, and, when he felt like it, clear as a fucking bell. Over the years, Charlie just got better and better at finding those moments and creating that seemingly time-stopping flurry, where the backbeat was exploded into a supernova of drums and vocals.

"Loving Cup" on *Exile* was the pinnacle: everything that Charlie had learned from Earl Palmer, Bo Diddley, Jimmy Miller, and Charlie Mingus's free-spirit of a drummer, Dannie Richmond, had been sown into this field of R&B, gospel, and outer-space kung fu. It was practically a throwback to the counterpunches thrown against the easygoing meter of "You Can't Always Get What You Want," but with all of the hippie optimism excised. Notwithstanding the funky, New Orleans–style soul groove and the killer outro, Charlie's incredible rock 'em, sock 'em tattoo when Mick hit the chorus was the real highlight of the show. It was modern dance on the drums, mixing time signatures by adding a beat to keep Mick floating on the first bit, *"Give me little drink …"* before falling back into the groove, and then opening it up again with the oddball timing when he delivers the next line, *"Just one drink …"*

Switching time signatures from bar to bar is the kind of thing you'd expect from insecure prog-rockers, too clever by half. But in Charlie's hands, it was completely organic. It kicked hard, but it flowed easily, and even as it was happening it was hard to see exactly where it was going to land. But there was never a feeling that anything weird was going on, unless, course, you tried to play it—it was advanced shit, for black belts and beyond, mind-curdling for any amateur trying to cop the lick without getting lost in the added beat. But I've already told you the secret: *when you are playing the melody, you don't have to count.*

Charlie, who had never taken a single drum lesson, a jazz cat who didn't have the chops to play like his jazz heroes—he didn't have the left hand that could skittle along on the snare drum, creating a seamless flow of alternating urgency and playfulness like his drumming heroes Philly Joe or Tony Williams—was creating new ways to get inside the song, climbing right up into the guts of the thing and spilling them out for everyone to see. It may not have been pretty, but it sure was beautiful. Such was the world of the Rolling Stones.

○ ○ ○

Charlie was doing a bit of freelancing in those years, first sitting in on Leon Russell's self-titled LP, playing on a track along with Bill Wyman. Which might have seemed like quite the coup, getting the Rolling Stones' rhythm section to play on your record, except not only did he have Charlie and Bill, he also had Mick singing, not to mention half of the Beatles on a handful of tunes, what with George and Ringo joining the fray. Leon Russell always had a lot of heavy friends.

Anyway, aside from it being a swell record, *Leon Russell* is that lovely anomaly of Charlie and Ringo splashing around in the same pond. One of the really great things to come out of this session was an early version of "Shine a Light," then titled "(Can't Seem to) Get a Line on You," a couple of years before it appeared on *Exile*, and sung by Mick—Leon Russell relegates himself to piano—with Bill on bass and Ringo on the drums, a remarkable collision of talent. If you wanted to see how Ringo and Charlie handled the same song, well, this was *not* your chance, because remember, Jimmy Miller played on "Shine a Light." Still, if you wanted to hear Ringo playing with the Stones, this was as close as you were going to get, and he does a wonderful job of keeping the gospel-soul groove with his own slightly unbalanced fills and solid feel.

More telling are the songs that Ringo plays on that call for a deep blues pocket: "Shoot Out on the Plantation" and "Hurtsome Body" are so loaded up with Ringo-isms—heavy on the bass drum, too many frills on the hi-hat—the kind of stuff that worked on later Beatles records, but ultimately fail here, more or less killing any chance the songs had of swinging, whereas Charlie's playing on "Roll Away the Stone," admittedly a straightforward affair, seems to lift the entire song.

As it is, it's a good reminder that the Beatles were never going to be the Stones any more than the Stones were going to be the Beatles (despite a few attempts at trying), and if you were wondering if Ringo and Charlie were playing the same game, all you had to do is go back and listen to the Beatles play "Kansas City," which in their hands sounds lite and white, or "Revolution," which is properly heavy (oh, that guitar sound!) and drives along on something like a shuffle beat, but with a bass drum that would kill any legit blues number, throbbing more than swinging. A cool drum part, to be sure—*boom pa boom papa boom!*—but it wasn't the kind of thing that would have cut it in Chicago.

Another record featuring Charlie Watts and Bill Wyman came out in 1971, a bagatelle called the *London Howlin' Wolf Sessions*. It was actually a very enjoyable record (if not nearly as profound as an original slab of Howlin' Wolf cut in Chicago or Memphis), and a nice chance for Bill and Charlie to sit down with one of the Stones' great heroes, and, for the rest of us, to hear them have some fun away from the madding crowd of Mick and Keith.[5]

It was a hustle, of course, a cash grab to build a pseudo-supergroup and get Eric Clapton and a couple of guys from the Stones together (not to mention Steve Winwood, who overdubbed his parts at a later date)—how could they resist making a record with Howlin' Wolf? Why, it would have been selfish not to!

And this, too, was that *avis raris*, a record that Charlie and Ringo both play on.

Ringo only made it onto one track on the final record, "I

---

5 Speaking of being away from Keith, Keith's inability to get out of bed one evening (read into that what you will) led to an artifact that eventually became known as *Jamming with Edward*, a session at Olympic Studios featuring the rest of the Stones, Charlie, Bill, and Mick, plus piano man Nicky Hopkins and bottleneck guitar ace Ry Cooder, who had been along to help out in the wake of Brian leaving (but eventually left, bitter that his work had been largely uncredited, a story for another book, perhaps). Anyway, the band, even featuring three official Stones, plus as good a guitar player and piano player as anyone could imagine, sounded perfectly toothless without Keith. It sounds *vaguely* like the Stones, largely due to Charlie, whose personal style shines throughout, and of course Mick's voice, but it's all spaghetti and no meatballs—so much, in fact, that when the Stones had the temerity to put out this waste of perfectly good recording tape as a long-playing phonograph record, it came with a disclaimer from Mick: "I hope you spend longer listening to this record than we did recording it." One odd thing worth noting: Bill plays much differently when Keith isn't around, moving without the same subtlety that he minted in the Stones, humping his way though the changes, and stepping out in front here and there with the kind of shit that would have brought Keith's switchblade leaping from his pocket. It's a funny business, this band stuff, who is and who is not replaceable, not to mention the influence heavy objects have on other objects near them.

Ain't Superstitious," which he attacks with an unnecessary funk, the kind of thing that was pure genius on "Come Together" or "Ticket to Ride," but which is basically a drag on a down and dirty blues. Everything Charlie touches, of course, rolls right along. Not to overstate it, but the difference in drummers *tells*, and it's pretty good proof that Ringo wouldn't have lasted five minutes in the Rolling Stones. Which is not to say that Charlie is a better drummer than Ringo—because, really, who cares?—but, rather, just a friendly reminder that playing the drums is all about *context*.

o o o

Finally, *penetration.*

The aggressiveness and focus that was gained between the 1969 tour and their outings over the next few years was a giant leap for mankind.

In 1969, the Stones had easily graduated to the head of their class. They were something to be enjoyed, and even marveled at. Within the next couple of years, they were something to be *feared*, gangsters so in control of their own destiny, so unapologetic and unremitting in their attack, that anyone who was in the same line of work had to stop and question just what the hell they were doing, and if there were any real point in carrying on.

A certain agent in this change was the addition of the all-Texas horn section—Bobby Keys and Jim Price—who helped turn THE GREATEST ROCK'N'ROLL BAND IN THE WORLD into a vicious, uncompromising soul revue, overcharged and badass. The horns sounded like they were kidnapped at knifepoint from Muscle Shoals and reprogrammed personally by Keith Richards, shot up with military grade amphetamine—pure crystal, no biker crank, the good stuff, the shit that won wars. The whole crew looked like they were about to rob a pharmacy.

Charlie, as ever, was the most levelheaded of the bunch. He was an odd sort of rock star—one who was more likely to be found listening to Count Basie than snorting drugs—and preferred to stay out of the limelight when he wasn't working. When the band went to a party at the Playboy Mansion, he famously spent his time playing pinball while the rest of the Stones frolicked—they were a cadre of girl-happy, picaresque, drug enthusiasts and fashionistas who couldn't stay out of the news, but as long as they played with the conviction of successful serial killers, they could afford to flaunt their lifestyles.[6] Onstage, when Keith was *too* fucked up or got *too* loose, when Mick was too busy strutting to properly work the mic, no one cared. In fact, it only added to their mystique and high sense of danger, skirting the edges of chaos and control. But the drummer enjoyed no such luxury, he never would. If Charlie missed a beat or came down missing the "one," everyone in the house would know it. If the drums stopped, it would be a disaster, the Walls of Jericho tumbling down.

Charlie's style was seemingly uncomplicated, but it was impossible to duplicate. He was an enlightened savant, unchained. His unique, old-world sense of syncopation and newfound futurist frenzy pushed the Rolling Stones over the top into an unparalleled stratum of audacity, courage, and revolt, and his unwavering commitment to the song created a wily launching pad for the singer, who sang and spat with more soul than he ever did, before or after.

The difference between "Stray Cat Blues" in 1969 and "Stray Cat Blues" in 1971 was the difference between kittens playing under a blanket and feral cougars eating their young. Mick snarls. Charlie shows his claws. The horns purr.

"Live with Me," recorded live at the Roundhouse in London in '71, on their brief tour of the UK, is as stunning a four minutes of pure rock'n'soul as ever recorded, with Nicky Hopkins leading

---

6 Jazz, blues, rock, whatever, Duke Ellington summed it up when he declared, "It's like an act of murder; you play with intent to commit something."

the band in on the piano—revealing the song's secret boogie roots, an epiphany of sorts, since the concept of anything as friendly as a rolling piano is not so evident on the studio version—before the guitar lick takes over with another post-"Satisfaction" bit of riff-bashing, the sort of thing that would become the foundation of all hard rock to follow.[7]

The horns scream, honk, and wail. Mick sings and shouts about meat and whores, water rats, and French maids being fucked behind pantry doors. How could anything be so *sexy* and so *brutal* all at once?

This was the magic time, the perfect nexus of art, drugs, and eyeliner, and if Richard Nixon were on his game, he would have put a stop to it. This was rock'n'roll run amok in a very real, very ugly way, an assault on the establishment and everything that was decent. It was the covenant of rock'n'roll fulfilled.

To watch *Ladies and Gentlemen: The Rolling Stones*, the document of their 1972 American tour to promote *Exile*, is to see a group hit a level of excellence that has never been equaled, twisting blues and rock'n'roll and jump and jive and utter sleaze into a symphony of boogie-woogie, sex, glam rock, and violence, and it could never have been done without a drummer who didn't have the roll part of the equation coursing through his veins, who wasn't obsessed with jazz and swing and big bands. There were groups that played *heavier*, but no one played *harder*, or with such

---

7 Frequently bootlegged, the Stones officially released this, along with a generous dose of other equally slashing live tracks and outtakes, on the deluxe reissue of *Sticky Fingers*.

riveting primacy and confidence—the Who and Led Zeppelin sounded downright *rococo* next to the Stones' highly distilled strain of mayhem.

"Street Fighting Man" as it was delivered in the studio could never be duplicated, not by five guys with tawdry electric guitars and drums, so onstage the Stones ripped it apart—acoustic guitar had given way to the Big Electric Riff. The bass rumbled like something more meteorological than purely musical, and where there once was a stoic campaign on the drums, there was now a violent flurry of hi-hats splattering the chorus, crash cymbals exploding like incendiary devices pasting the upbeat, rapid-fire rolls and military snare-drum drills pushing the end of the song into the realm of a genuine uprising—it was the rock'n'roll equivalent of a student riot. That the police didn't come with fire hoses and teargas the second Keith played the opening riff had to be some kind of grand oversight by law enforcement.

The Stones were having their way with the history of rock'n'roll, and had come so far along that they were now deconstructing and rebuilding their own strategic attacks, seemingly in the moment. When they dropped "Rip This Joint" on *Exile on Main St.*, the fastest song in their catalogue, Charlie was content to romp through the breaks, swinging hard, but not breaking any boundaries. But now, live, after living with it for a few months, he was having at it with the savage expressionism of a modern dancer schooled in African tribalism and extraterrestrial semaphore. It was a new language, as yet unheard of in what had begun as a hard jump and jive:

"RIP THIS JOINT"
WHAM, BAM, BIRMINGHAM....

STUDIO VERSION eeeeeeee

LIVE! ☆♫♪♩♪☆◎☆!♩

Charlie was shifting time and space to create this new reality—
"Midnight Rambler" clocked in at anywhere between nine and
thirteen minutes on those tours, depending, I suppose, on the
amount of drugs Keith took before the show, and how much fun
Mick was having taunting the audience, and no song in history has
ever explored with such offhand grace and atavistic primitivism
Delta hoodoo, city blues, and impossibly swank shuffles, and
conflated so many incongruous vibes: *Let's boogie! I'm the Boston
Strangler! I'm going to stab you! Suck my cock! Let's boogie some more!*

"Midnight Rambler" floated in easily enough with a lascivious
but laid-back shuffle, the kind of thing the Stones had been
perfecting since day one, except here they were pushing it closer
and closer to the line, accelerating and gradually increasing in
intensity—*anticipation!*—before it took off like a rocket into an oily,
unconstrained, four-on-the-floor romp that traversed the difference
between "blues" and "rock," a spectacular bit of drumming that,
along with Keith's guitar, tuned regular but capo'd at the seventh fret
for extra tension, took everyone along on a giddy murder spree.

Never mind "Helter Skelter"—as charming as it was, it didn't
swing. "Midnight Rambler," though, was jazz in every sense. It had

charisma. It had *magnetism.* It had *depth.* It was *sexy,* and it had the dangerous edge of improvisation, echoing the tempo changes of Mingus and his hard-rolling drummer, Dannie Richmond, who could shred music for prayer meetings and exotic fight songs with the same sort of wild abandon.

"Midnight Rambler" wasn't so much a song as it was a *crime scene.* Charlie drops accents like shell casings. Mick sounds like he is choking the life out of the harmonica. He free-associates about oral sex. Strains of Chicago and the Mississippi Delta rise up like steam. The message was terrible, all about rape and murder.

When the song breaks down, women are screaming. It's hard to tell if they are turned on or scared. Likely a little bit of both. Once upon a time, there was a cute ad campaign: *Would you let your daughter marry a Rolling Stone?* In these years, a better question would have been: *Why the hell weren't they in jail?*

Gustav Mahler, who once proclaimed that the symphony must encompass the world, would have stopped, looked, and listened, had he been confronted with this suite of menace and ecstatic hoodoo. He probably would have written a redemptive final movement for these cats. Someday, I am sure somebody will.

Muddy Waters, as restless as the deep blue sea.
(Photofest)

SIX

THE "V" WORD

IT WAS MUDDY WATERS WHO LET ME KNOW that I had been lied to.

It was about a week after I had gone to see Jeff Beck at the old Palladium on 14th Street in Manhattan, a field trip I now blame on the fog of war that is high school and marijuana, and the received wisdom that Jeff Beck was some sort of GOD, part of a Holy Trinity that included Eric Clapton and Jimmy Page, all former inmates in the Yardbirds—who, despite their own debatable virtues, proved to be some sort of incubator for guitar talent, at least if you accept that everyone who had the gig went on to bigger and (and in the case of Page, anyway) better things.

Beck fulfilled his own promise—the whole act was architected to prove his primacy as a guitar hero. He articulated complete mastery over his Stratocaster, painting the room with a full spectrum of colors, squeezing out sonic hot flashes of varying intensity, alternately squealing like wounded animals and orgasmic women, and all from what has to be considered a primitive musical instrument, because, after all, what is an electric guitar but a piece of wood with a few magnets drilled into it?

But primitivism is something Beck would never understand, and as such, unlike his colleague Jimmy Page, neither would he ever understand that while rock was about the guitar, roll was about the drums.

I remember a thing called "Space Boogie," which promised to combine two of my very favorite motifs and delivered on neither, boogie being something you can dance to, and space being a place I'd like to go. Instead we got clobbered with a double-bass-drum workout that left little doubt about the drummer's cardiovascular superiority but not much else, and a guitar played through some sort of synthesizer, a whole lot of flash designed to dazzle, but no real song.

Beck ended his set with "Going Down" (the number made famous by Freddie King and something of a Beck signature, not to be confused with the excellent Stones outtake "I'm Going Down"), which in his hands sounded very similar to actual rock'n'roll, but on closer inspection failed the test. There was neither *anticipation* nor *penetration*, just *ejaculation*.[1]

---

1 Which reminds me of the only two times I've ever seen Charlie Watts look completely annoyed behind the drum set. The first was when they played Hyde Park in 1969, the first show with Mick Taylor, a few days after Brian Jones died. The guitars are woefully out of tune, and they are deboning "Satisfaction" at a maddening, half-cooked tempo. Charlie is doing his best to pile-drive some life into

o o o

Which brings us to Muddy Waters.

A few months after the Jeff Beck show, I trundled up to the Beacon Theatre on the Upper West Side to see Muddy Waters. Like a lot of folks, I had found the blues through the Rolling Stones. They loved Muddy Waters, therefore I should, too. Transitive theory and all that.

Anyway, there I was at the Beacon, smoking more or less the same weed as I was at the Jeff Beck ta-do, although this time I was sharing it with a well-dressed, middle-aged black couple, and not some suburban burnout in a Hot Tuna T-shirt.[2] And it should be noted that Muddy and Beck play very similar instruments—slabs of wood with magnets and wires—the crude building blocks of the electric guitar have never really changed.

---

the song, and can be seen in the film yelling "C'mon!" in frustration, and clearly not having any fun. The other time was when Jeff Beck sat in with them on their 2012 tour, to give "Going Down" a run, and the first sound to come out of Beck's guitar was the kind of McSquealy thingy that doesn't really have a place with the Rolling Stones, and ultimately, even with Mick doing the Mick thing, had little to do with the Stones—it was really just about Jeff Beck the Guitar Hero taking over for five impossibly long minutes, and Charlie looked completely steamed, like he was hating every second of it, just tempestuously smashing about on his cymbals. Keith was of no help, not even attempting to groove it—it seemed like he couldn't wait for the talent show to end, either. That being said, Charlie has only ever had nice things to say about Jeff Beck.

2 I pretended it was all normal, but I was secretly ecstatic to be that much closer to the culture. Later, I was thrilled to hear Mick tell a similar story, of visiting the Apollo on the Stones' first trip to New York, amazed because he had "never seen housewives smoke pot before."

Muddy pulled the greatest sound I had ever heard in my life out of his Telecaster—a looooong, lonely wail, the sound of space and time collapsing on top of each other, cries from the sweltering Mississippi Delta, both plaintive and pleading. *"They call me Muddy Waters,"* he sang. *"I'm just as restless as the deep blue sea."* His hands were enormous, he could barely get his finger through the copper tube he used as a bottleneck, and he filled the hall with perfect, primitive atavism, a single twisted note that spoke of lust and frustration and conquest, an uncompromised mating ritual—anticipation and penetration!—and that's when I had my epiphany. Much like the Apostle Paul, who once wrote in a letter to someone called the Corinthians, "When I was a child, I spoke and thought and reasoned as a child. But when I grew up, I put away childish things."

I was a witness. I saw and heard what moved Chuck Berry to worship this man. I felt what the Rolling Stones felt, what moved them to start playing the blues, and why they were never driven to play a zillion notes, just the *right* ones. Miles Davis had that going for him, too.

That Muddy Waters and Miles Davis were both virtuosos is inarguable, but some dimwitted muso is bound to argue that the V word signals a technical prowess of which neither was possessed: Muddy was an unschooled primitive with limited technique, and Miles, for all of his musical education and natural gifts, never played with blinding speed, and his range, like Frank Sinatra's or Billie Holiday's, was limited—no stratospheric high notes for those cats—but damn, they had an awful knack for hitting the *right* note, every fucking time. When it came to cutting through the bullshit and expressing pure human emotion, they were freakishly evolved.

I've heard it said that gifted people can hit targets that others can't reach, geniuses hit targets that others can't see. My favorite character in the *Peanuts* comic strip is Schroeder, the Beethoven obsessive who plays infinitely complex sonatas flawlessly, on a toy piano. One day, his friend Lucy says to him, "How can you play all those notes *when the black keys are just painted on?*"

"Practice."

Nowhere in the definition of "virtuoso" is it written that you have to play a lot of notes. Undeniably, Jeff Beck is a virtuoso guitar player, but he takes all the virtue out of virtuoso when he puts himself before the song. Just because you can make your guitar sound like a video arcade doesn't mean you should.

Perhaps you don't think the Ramones are virtuosos, but go ahead and try to play in that style *convincingly*—unless you are a student of the sport with a work ethic and skill set rivaling the United States Special Forces, chances are you won't last very long. I've heard all sorts of self-described musicians (mostly metal-heads, prog-rockers, humorless jazzers, and fusion nerds) claim with *authority* that punk rock isn't even music (??!!), or that *anyone* can play it, and I've seen guitar shredders and drummers with years of schooling and incredible technical skill give it a go, and the results are laughable. Ditto I've seen a million punk-rock bands, kids in torn jeans, black leather jackets, and Converse high-tops have at playing punk rock in the Ramones style, true apostles of the art form, and some of them are quite good, but only one in a million is good enough. Also, it takes four people who are vibrating at the exact same frequency. Good luck with that.

Music isn't an Olympic event, but every now and then degree of difficulty counts. The Ramones' music may sound simple, but they were the high priests of an art form they helped to create, and there isn't a rock band on the planet formed after they laid down their musical manifesto—an uncomplicated forward drive, free of syncopation—that wasn't somehow influenced by them.

You don't think minimalists can be virtuosos? Tell it to Hemingway. Tell it to Thelonious Monk. Tell it to the Japanese calligrapher who spends his entire life perfecting a straight line, or drawing a flawless circle.

The suburban male concept of virtuosity has conflated technical prowess with musical value. It worships complex recipes, not pure ingredients. It's a toxic system that rewards show-offs and neuters authentic folk musicians—meaning masters of their indigenous art, not the navel-gazing, guitar-strumming mold that seems to grow in every nook and cranny of the world's high-schools and colleges. I'm talking about folks like Muddy Waters or Bob Marley, Joseph Spence, or Ali Farka Touré. Virtuosity and simplicity need not be at odds.

Let me ask you this: if you are John Lennon, and you can call any drummer in the world to play on your first solo album, why call Ringo? Because John trusted him to bring out the full range of emotion in his songs, and boy-oh-boy was that some kind of widescreen psychodrama of a record, from "Mother" to "God," and Ringo made it all sound very natural, not forced, 100 percent organic. In between, he cast flawless parts for the rockers and garage numbers, bringing his understated funk and character to what would become Lennon's best record. So what if he couldn't cut it with Howlin' Wolf—Charlie Watts played great on a Pete Townshend side project, but it didn't mean he was even remotely qualified to play with the Who. With John Lennon and the Beatles, Ringo was not replaceable.

Everyone these days, it seems, is better at everything: hockey players, chess players, high jumpers, plumbers, you name it, the technology and education has improved incalculably over the years, as has the equipment, the training, and the reduced barrier to entry in every field. Music schools are turning out kids who can play at levels not imaginable when the Beatles or the Stones were coming up. It's easy to get your hands on an electric guitar these days. All you have to do is push a button and Chico Hamilton or Muddy Waters will come gushing out of your phone. No one is taking apart banjos to play the drums anymore.

Rush bulletin boards—that is, online discussions of the band Rush—are lousy with shithead comments like, "Can someone PLEASE explain Charlie Watts to me? He doesn't do anything I couldn't have done after one week of drum lessons," or, "Who are the luckiest drummers in the world?" And the *de facto* answer is always, "Ringo Starr, a talentless guy who made a fortune playing with *real musicians*."

And for every one of these know-nothings trying to look tall by standing on the head of someone more talented than they, there is always another dingbat who *should* know better, but just can't help himself—jerks like Aerosmith's drummer, Joey Kramer, who likes to boast how much better Aerosmith were than the Stones: "They never had anything to offer me musically, especially in the drumming department."

John Coltrane, and Jimi Hendrix (opposite) …

Which is ironic, because Kramer plays the drums in a band that had done their best to distill the better parts of the Rolling Stones, Led Zeppelin, and the New York Dolls— except that he had none of the finesse, imagination, or ability to swing that made Charlie Watts tops in his class; he lacked Bonham's rhythmic invention, power, technique, and fearlessness; and he didn't even come close to the natural swagger of Dolls drummer Jerry Nolan, who will never be as famous as the others, but whose drumming was the musical equivalent of a zip gun, leather jacket, and pegged pants. Which is why Aerosmith could only ever be a very good band, and never a great one, and why when I play the drums along with their records, I actually get *worse* —playing along with Kramer is like playing tennis with someone who lobs all the time.

Ringo gets slagged even by people who are celebrating him.

"Define 'best drummer in the world,'" former Nirvana drummer
Dave Grohl said in a *tribute* to Ringo. "Is it someone that's
technically proficient? Or is it someone that sits in the song with

their own feel?" Implying, of course
that Ringo was lacking in the technical
proficiency department, that he was
some kind of idiot savant, untrained
and working on instinct alone, which
is not only insulting, it is ridiculous,
and it is this sort of equivocation that
makes me want to hurl. Was Grohl
trying to protect his own reputation
as an accomplished drummer, or just
letting us know that he was in on the
joke, that Ringo really wasn't all that
good, but, you know, *The Beatles*?

The true virtuoso is a paragon of
humility. They aren't overly impressed
with themselves. The show-off feeds
on his own talent. They self-fellate
because they can. The true virtuoso

... in love with the universe. (Photofest)

has no need. Look at John Coltrane
or Jimi Hendrix—they were in torrid love affairs with the *universe*.
Their music made the world seem bigger.

Ol' Kittenish on the Keys, the unabashedly virtuosic popinjay
Liberace, if not the most serious musician ever to run his fingers
across the keys, used the gift God gave him simply to bring joy to

his audiences. Even covered in diamonds and furs, he projected an earthy humility—a remarkable talent in its own right, even if he weren't shredding impossible boogies and ramped up renditions of Chopin, perpetrating what he called "classical music with the boring parts left out," spinning the "Minute Waltz" in record time. No one ever left a Liberace performance without having absorbed some of his radiant charm.

o o o

Somewhere I read that virtuosity requires consistent, flawless excellence. Ease and comfort not only in difficult passages, but an ability to bring humanity and heart to the simplest ones. I thought that was pretty good.

Vic Firth is far more famous now for the drumstick manufacturer that bears his name than he was as a virtuoso timpanist for the Boston Symphony. But what does that really even mean, *virtuoso timpanist*? Ever hear long kettledrum workouts at the concert hall? There are more timpani parts in your average Phil Spector song than there are in an entire season of the Boston Symph. But when you are playing Beethoven's Symphony No. 7, or No. 9, and the time comes to hit those things, you had better be there, and without imparting any personal mojo into the part. Timpani can project a lot of emotion, *Sturm und Drang* or victory in the case of Beethoven, or cosmic coupling as in the case of Strauss, and it takes genuine, humane musicianship to deliver it, but you are always under the baton of another sort of virtuoso, playing a part written by yet another, and your opinion hardly matters. Being timpanist could mean dropping two hits in a score hundreds of pages long—that's a lot of time waiting around, and no smoking or drinking allowed—but you are there to execute, to deliver *exactly* what the score calls for, on time, with the precision of a space-shuttle launch, and not to go into business for yourself and dazzle with your wondrous technique. It's a lot different to the type of virtuosity enjoyed by Ella Fitzgerald or Frank Zappa, but if you're looking for a gig that begs for completely uncompromising and unselfish musical excellence in the cause of the greater good, this would be it.

More to the point, virtuosity is just a word. Say it enough and it doesn't mean anything. You can call a pie a cake, but it doesn't make it so, and anyone who thinks Jeff Beck or Buddy Rich offers more musical potency than Muddy Waters or Charlie Watts, solely based on the illusion of their instrumental prowess, is perversely wrong. It goes without question that THE GREATEST ROCK'N'ROLL BAND IN THE WORLD would need THE GREATEST ROCK'N'ROLL DRUMMER. But if you are asking who is "the best" drummer, you are asking the wrong question.

Live in Honolulu, 1973. (Robert Knight
Archives/Redferns/Getty Images)

SEVEN

THE HARDER
THEY COME

THE GIGANTIC HI-HAT *shwoop* that signaled the opening of *Goats Head Soup*, the Stones' 1973 follow-up to *Exile on Main St.*, felt an awful lot like a drug bust.

The sound of the opening and closing hi-hat—*shwoop!*—had become the signifier of something bigger than itself: a brand of sex that was both elegant and illicit, a lifestyle far removed from any hippie dream.

Isaac Hayes and Curtis Mayfield had been doing wonderful things, driving *Shaft* and *Superfly* straight outta Harlem with two-fisted *shucka-wucka* hi-hat riffs and well-greased wah-wah pedals. They made those chatter cymbals sound like crime in the city. Pretty soon, porn movies and even SWAT teams copped the same oily sound for their soundtracks—everybody wanted a part of it.

John Bonham knew how to use the hi-hat like a magician—just

listen to how he announced himself on the first song on the first Zep record, "Good Times Bad Times"—and then he put the *ching-ring* tambourine gimmick on the hi-hat to drive "Moby Dick," *changchangchangchangchang*. It sounded like an ice-cream man on speed, making change for an army of hopped up schoolchildren.

Keith Moon was so overwhelmed with the two million drums he had surrounded himself with that he didn't even bother with his hi-hat.

Charlie made the hi-hat *his* thing, lighting it up behind the singer to sell the song. It was his own strain of jazz, and it took some macho and imagination, though it was always more music than muscle. It was that famous Watts right hand that delivered the knockout punch, but it took a suave touch to find the right space.

Goats Head Soup was a pointedly more urban sound than the Stones had been perpetrating until then, a low sort of funk that took the Stones through a glass, darkly.[1] The gleeful decadence of "Rocks Off" and "Rip this Joint" that had announced *Exile's* extended splatter painting of roots music had evaporated. This was their first record that sounded less like *inspiration*, and more like *obligation*.

Keith's problems with the law were as epic as his drug problem—they began recording *Goats Head Soup* at the end of 1972 at Dynamic Sound Studios in Kingston, Jamaica, not so much by choice, but because there weren't too many other places that would have them. "Jamaica was one of the few places that would let us

---

1 "Your brain is going to run out of your ears when you get a hold of *Goats Head Soup!*"—from a television ad voiced by DJ Wolfman Jack.

all in," Keith recounts in the Stones' oral history. "Nine countries kicked me out, thank you very much, so it was a matter of how to keep this thing together …"

Dynamic Sound, where they set up to make this record, was a far cry from their safe European home. The entrance was a large gate flanked by armed guards, and the gear was nailed to the floor so no one would swipe it. Such was Kingston in 1972, which makes it no surprise that one of the best original gangsta movies of them all, *The Harder They Come*, a story about a cop killer–turned–pop star, was filmed there. The soundtrack—a Keith obsession, and the first great beacon of reggae music to the hip world—was largely recorded at Dynamic.

Which may well have made it a romantic proposition to Keith, who would eventually fall so in love with Jamaica that he basically moved there, but for the moment he was a bad junkie, working in the long shadow of *Exile on Main St.* and the world-beating tour that followed, struggling to conjure up enough juju to fill two sides of a long-player.

° ° °

All great artists struggle as they mature. Coltrane was a disciple of Charlie Parker before he exploded with his own thing, rocketing from sheets of sound to *A Love Supreme* to a brand of outer-space jazz that few could understand. It took David Bowie a few records just to realize he actually *was* from outer space. Ornette Coleman got beaten up and his saxophone trashed in Baton Rouge for playing R&B in a style not to the liking of the locals, before he changed the rules of harmony, melody, and rhythm, and helped invent "free jazz," only to get beaten up by crusty jazz purists who couldn't make sense of his work, either. Dalí's early stuff looked like Van Gogh, Picasso's like Raphael or one of the other Ninja Turtles, and then all of a sudden clocks started dripping from trees and women started showing up with two eyes on the same side of their heads. And so it was with the Rolling Stones. They began as a covers band and grappled uneasily with writing songs, and then suddenly it was all about that crossfire hurricane, maracas, and a string of hits. But they flew too close to the sun.

Keith told *Creem* magazine, "I started going my way—which was the downhill road to Dopesville—and Mick ascended to Jetland."

It's not easy being in a band, even when everyone is taking the same drugs. But it gets weird fast when you all start sleeping with the same women, and people start turning up dead in swimming pools, and the guitar player is an unrepentant dope fiend, who, when he wasn't nodding out or otherwise strung out (or dodging the law, or locked in his room shivering and shaking), was flying on coke and speed, staying up for days on end (his record would be an impressive nine days, no sleep), working frantically, drinking more whisky than Charles Bukowski and Jerry Lee Lewis combined, and, bless his soul, *making it work*.

Meanwhile, the singer's love affair with himself showed no signs of slowing down—dizzy with stardom and floating in a whorl of fashion and trendy sexuality, still trying to find himself, even after proving himself as a lyricist and vocalist of profound depth and emotion, an entertainer and rock'n'roll front man without equal, the *exemplar* of what a rock star should be, he was still never sure whether to tart up or go butch.

Charlie was something like the straight man in a British sitcom—the sympathetic glue between the druggy, heavily armed, pirate-like guitar player and the gender-bending lead singer, which is yet one more reason Why Charlie Watts Matters: he came to play. Keith and Mick weren't always a sure thing at these sessions, and when Bill had enough with this sort of childish idiocy he just fucked off and let Keith fill in on bass while he waited for the next tour to start. But Charlie had become a mereological essential to the group, the axis around which the Rolling Stones revolved.

Charlie and Mick, 1975, like a great British sitcom. (Christopher Simon Sykes/Hulton Archive/Getty Images)

You could listen to any of the last Stones records and know instantly who it was, *just from the drums*. You could hear it in the loping, behind-the-riff combinations of snare and tom-tom on "Monkey Man" on *Let It Bleed*. It was all over *Sticky Fingers*— no one else would have even imagined playing the intro and the fills on "Sway" like Charlie Watts did. The turnarounds on "Bitch" and the relentless outro of "Brown Sugar," just like those great moments on "Loving Cup" and the outburst at the beginning of "All Down the Line," were loose and mean. The backbeat had become monstrous both in power and nuance, chasing Keith as he did with the snare drum, jabbing with ghost notes and mini–buzz rolls that anticipated the downbeat. Like a prizefighter, he knew how to feint and jab, and then drop the big right hook.

Don Was, who would later become the Stones' producer and work on remastering *Exile*, proclaimed that "if *Exile* proves anything, it's that you can put Charlie Watts in a dank basement or the best recording studio on earth and he's going to sound like Charlie Watts."

"There's nothing forced about Charlie," Keith told *Rolling Stone*, "least of all his modesty. It's *totally* real. He cannot understand what people see in his drumming."

o o o

Singers had it easy. They came out of the womb crying, and the good ones figured it out from there. Of course, in the history of music there have been few great *stylists*—true originals—but there was no mistaking one great voice for another ...

ROBERT PLANT, CARMEN MIRANDA
JANIS JOPLIN, AL JOLSON
FRANK SINATRA, HANK WILLIAMS
LITTLE RICHARD, JAMES BROWN
ELVIS PRESLEY, BOB DYLAN, JOHNNY CASH
ARETHA FRANKLIN, BILLIE HOLIDAY, ETC., ETC.

And guitar players, too, although it took a lot more heavy lifting and innovation than just pushing air ...

BO DIDDLEY, CHUCK BERRY, KEITH RICHARDS
JOHN LEE HOOKER, POPS STAPLES
ELMORE JAMES, B.B. KING
LINK WRAY, PETE TOWNSHEND
JIMI HENDRIX, EDDIE VAN HALEN, ETC., ETC.

But drummers, not so much.

Keith Moon, like Charlie Watts, had become a great drummer by breaking every rule that drummers were normally taught about technique and tempo, whereas John Bonham did everything *right*—his technique was virtuosic, his concept of rock'n'roll, of *anticipation* and *penetration*, was not only impeccable and complex, but far more advanced than anyone who had straddled the snare drum before him.

Bonham also knew well the elusive nature of time: *The Swiss made it! The Americans said it was money! The Italians squandered it! Indians said it didn't exist!* What was this thing *time*?

Well, it was something for drummers to manipulate: speed up when you felt like you needed to step on the gas, slow down when it added *anticipation*. Time was something very fuckwithable.

Well, for drummers who were simply *good*, maybe not so much— but the *great* ones, hell yes. Listen to Bonham on "Kashmir"—the tempos shift constantly throughout the song. The verses push, the choruses pull.

Moon, of course, had little interest in the conventional notion of timekeeping—for the Who, it was more about momentum. But Charlie, too, knew that time was elastic.

Keith Richards told *Modern Drummer* about a session in the 1980s: "At the studio there was all this hi-tech stuff creeping in, and cats are working with click tracks and all that. We did a couple of run-throughs with this little machine. Charlie and I were looking at each other, because we *know*, but he had to beat the machine. He said, 'You want it like that? Here goes,' and he duplicated the click track tempo from the beginning of the song to the end of it, perfect, then he said, 'Now what it should do is come up a little bit in tempo here, and then it should pull back there.' … That's what Charlie knows innately, and that's why I love him."

You know the old joke? How do you know when a drummer is knocking at your door? *They speed up!* But a great drummer can accelerate with finesse, and when it is done right, not only wasn't it a problem, it got you really hot and bothered, to the point where you'd let pretty much anyone in.

Slow is good, too. A good song will tell you what to do. Sometimes Sinatra sang so far behind the beat that the band had packed up and gone home while he was still singing the bridge. But the women stuck around. They got it.

Lovers who have ever been chained to the damp groove of Al Green's simple Southern soul and funk know the sexual satisfaction that comes with rhythm done right. Technically speaking, there is nothing played on the drums on those songs— "Let's Stay Together," "I'm Still in Love with You," "Here I Am

(Come and Take Me)"—that someone with very little experience shouldn't be able play. Like a lot of simple soul and pop songs, if you can count to four, you should be able to have a go at it. But that tempo lives in a very profound place in the human erogenous zone, and good luck translating it to the grooves of a record.

There was only one man who could do it: Al Jackson, Jr., who kept the groove for Al Green and a bevy of other soul men and women—he was the Stax house drummer, the man who kept the groove for Booker T. and the M.G.'s—his super-simplified, brisk swing on "Green Onions" still confounds drummers

The New Urban Soul Men, Denmark, 1973.
(Globe Photos/Media Punch/Alamy)

who *think* they know how to play it, relying on their memory of hearing it on a TV commercial or in a movie, and then drag it into the ground with extra notes. His beats with Otis Redding—who called him "the world's greatest drummer"—are instantly recognizable, pushing the tempo almost imperceptibly, without ever leaving the pocket. But he never went as deep as those classic Al Green tracks. Those songs were hot, but they were also *slow*. "Al Jackson was probably ten times simpler than I am," Charlie Watts once marveled. "To be able to play as slow as Al Jackson is almost impossible ..."

The rhythm on those records sweats without rocking, percolates without ever boiling over, and, when he opened and closed the hi-hat, it was almost intolerably erotic.[2]

o o o

Charlie's open and closed hi-hats should have *elevated* "Dancing with Mr. D," the first cut on *Goats Head Soup*, but the whole thing was such a colossal bummer it was too heavy for anyone to lift, what with Keith's laconic, druggie funk riff and Mick's overwrought drawling about murder by guns and poison. If the best parts of *Exile* sounded *black*, the best song on *Goats Head Soup* sounded more like *Blaxploitation*.

"Doo Doo Doo Doo Doo (Heartbreaker)" was a good shot at the new sound of urban soul, with lyrics ripped from some imaginary headlines, some fiction about a child being shot. Good dance groove. Great chorus, but a total buzzkill of a message. *Anticipation* had turned to *desperation*. Such was the state of things that the bass player could hardly be bothered to show up to play on the new record—Bill Wyman is only on four songs on *Goats Head Soup*.

"Silver Train" was adequate. It was good, even. It provided four minutes of solid Stonesisms—a cool Keith riff driving along with Charlie right behind him, some decent slide guitarring from Mick No. 2, and Mick No. 1 doing that Mick thing and blowing some very decent harp—and if you loved the sound of the Stones, this was very much that, but you didn't have too get to close to see that

---

2 Al Jackson was murdered in 1975. It's amazing anyone ever got laid again.

they were wading through a swamp of their own effluence. Still, Stones crap was better than most folks' gold.

And no matter if Mick's head was in the stars, and no matter if Keith's head was in the sand or in the clouds, or some indeterminate place in between—in the loo shooting up, or getting sick, wherever it is that heroin takes one on good days or bad—at least you could count on Charlie to put the song over.

"Angie" was weak tea, a sprawling, chick-friendly ballad about breaking up, but the saddest thing about it was that it was never going to be "Wild Horses," anymore than "Silver Train" was going to be "All Down the Line," no matter how hard it tried. But it is as good a bit of drumming on a pop ballad as you were ever going to find, with all the Charlie Watts hallmarks intact—the loosey-goosey fills and the just-behind-the-beat groove that made it more genuinely *unctuous* than just melty and soft, because a song this saccharine could just have as easily turned into a puddle of goo if Charlie didn't bring the soul. And he delivered it in quantity, soul to *burn*, popping the hi-hat like the top of a bottle of ginger beer, effortless, effervescent, but also just *slightly* vindictive. That was part of the Stones sound, too—the musical equivalent of killing someone with a smile on your face.

The oddball in this mess was the sleeper hit, "Starfucker," a.k.a. "Star Star" (although the Stones themselves generally referred to it only as the former), and the most shocking thing about it—never mind the bits about pornographic Polaroids and the unrepentant fellating of famous movie stars, no biggie for a band that had already rhapsodized about cocksucking and sodomy-by-billy-club—was that it was quite dirty, both lyrically *and* musically, which isn't that easy to do.

The intro was a hot tease, like a natural blonde who dyes her roots dark to look cheap. Charlie's drums were so out of time against Keith's riff that it had to be some sort of inside joke, because certainly no band of this stature, or any stature, would leave something like that on a record, even if the song was about balling John Wayne—unless, of course, it was part of the gag.

The rest of the song is the Stones doing the Stones, and for a change Bill showed up to play bass, *but not until the second verse*, when he joins the party already in progress. It's quite something, actually—the song gets harder and faster as it goes along—it's all there, in its sloppiest, sluttiest, Stonesiest form, and, as tawdry as it is, has got to be considered a win in an otherwise rough season. It was never going to be "Gimme Shelter," but sense of humor in these things counts too, you know.

o o o

The follow-up LP was another near miss.

The title track, "It's Only Rock 'n Roll (But I Like It)" was an instant classic, but let's be honest, it doesn't come close to a good T. Rex song, and it doesn't even have Charlie on it for that extra bit of *zork*—it was recorded at Ron Wood's house, where he was working on his solo album, and surrounded by his best mates, including Kenney Jones, still of the Faces, on drums; Willie Weeks on bass; David Bowie, who sang backups; and of course Mick Jagger, who came in with the lyric and got Ron to help him finish this number and agreed to help out with Ron on a thing called "I Can Feel the Fire." At the end of the night, Mick says, "I'll Take 'It's Only Rock 'n Roll,' you keep the other." The Stones had a go at re-recording it, but in the end decided just to clean it up and rebuild the original track done at Ronnie's joint (as when Jimmy Miller sat in a few times, there were no complaints from Charlie, who felt that those guys were working hard to sound like him anyway, so why be bothered). Keith stabbed it with Chuck Berry riffs, Ian Stewart played the piano, Mick worked up the vocals, *et voila*, Big Hit. Naturally, the songwriting credit went to Jagger and Richards, such was the hustle. And this is how the stars line up for the Rolling Stones, even as they are in complete disarray.

If "It's Only Rock 'n Roll" was a one-off with two of the Faces sounding more like the Stones than the Faces normally did (which is saying a lot), but "Dance Little Sister" and "If You Can't Rock Me," the hardest rockers from the new effort, were pure Charlie and Keith—Keith busting out on the guitar, and Charlie chasing him.

"The whole heart and soul of this band is Keith and Charlie," Bobby Keys explained in *Life*. "I mean, that's apparent to anyone who's breathing or has a musical bone in his body. This is where the engine room is."

Mick spit the songs with perfect authority, but for now at least he was done writing anything of any relevancy too far beyond "*Hey, let's party*," or, "*Hey, watch me move*," and while the record had a few nice, largely forgotten moments—the underrated, rocksteady-like "Luxury," a sound version of the Temptations' "Ain't Too Proud to Beg," and a couple of passable ballads—they no longer sounded like young men. They sounded meaner on *Goats Head Soup*. No matter, as Jimmy Page had famously said about Keith, "You only have to put on 'Dance Little Sister' and you forgive the guy for anything."

It had been a long road for them—twelve or so years of hard work, from teenybopper idols to counterculture rebels and musical heavyweights with no real competition, to dawdling rock monarchy with nasty habits. They danced with dead bodies, bad drugs, good drugs, good women, bad women, outlaws of every stripe, and increasingly threatening run-ins with law enforcement, and the muse was getting crispy to the point of crumbling.

They had a great tour of Europe in 1973, supporting *Goats Head Soup*—a lot of the magic from the last tour was still in the air—but Bobby Keys was gone halfway through, dancing with his own heroin habit (though officially canned for that stunt with the Dom Pérignon and the bathtub), and it hurt—Bobby was Keith's running mate, and the best man at Mick's wedding.

But you know, he wasn't a broom, just a broom handle, and so it goes.

Goats Head Soup would also be the last Stones record for Jimmy Miller, who had joined Keith on the road to Dopesville back at *Nellcôte*, and had basically mainlined himself out of a gig. He didn't last long enough to even get his name on the record—production credits went to Mick and Keith's joint pseudonym, "The Glimmer Twins."

"Things get a little blurry here, " Keith confesses in *According to the Rolling Stones*. "I have only to go by the producers and how they died. Jimmy Miller was still there for *It's Only Rock 'n Roll*, because I remember him being down at Island Studios in London, but by then Jimmy was down to carving swastikas in the desk, bless his heart. He had assumed that he could adapt my lifestyle after a while, but he hadn't realized that my diet is very rare."

Jimmy was exactly the guy they had needed. He understood them. He had coached four great seasons for them, from *Beggars Banquet* and *Let It Bleed* to *Exile on Main St.* and *Sticky Fingers*, often considered the best run in the history of the sport, before the darkness of *Goats Head Soup* began their descent. He helped turn Charlie from a very good drummer to a truly great drummer. In fact, everyone had gotten better at what they did, and whether it was the Jimmy Miller influence or just their natural ascent, it was remarkable. But it was time to move on.[3]

And then Mick Taylor quit, just like that, telling Mick he was going to move on while they were having a drink at a party. He wasn't satisfied—he wanted to write songs, or some such piffle, and figured maybe he'd be better off without the Stones, since he, too, was now a ROCK STAR, with all of the *accouterments*, including his very own shiny heroin habit and newly minted shitty attitude.

According to one version of the story, Mick shrugged and looked over at Ronnie Wood, who of course was also at the party,

---

3 Post-Stones, Jimmy Miller went on to work with Johnny Thunders; co-produced one excellent record for Motörhead, *Overkill*, and another, *Bomber*, on which he was largely absent but heralded by bandleader Lemmy Kilmister for his "marvelous" junkie lies; the Plasmatics' debut, for which he was almost immediately fired for being too strung out on drugs to be functional; and, finally, Primal Scream's mesmerizing masterpiece *Screamadelica*, a certified classic, his last record before dying at the age of fifty-two from liver failure.

and asked if he'd fill in for the next tour. Ronnie shrugged and said "sure," why not.

o o o

Well, that's the short of it. There are books and movies all about it, but there it is. Keith didn't seem too upset. He admired Mick Taylor's talent but questioned his heart, and, anyway, turns out Mick Taylor wasn't that much fun to hang around with.

Losing Taylor actually loosened them up. He was never *truly* one of them, he was just the player they needed to win a few more championships—the gifted power forward who was going to score some big goals and end up becoming a free agent at the end of a few seasons, no matter what.

For the moment, Ronnie was only signed on to tour with the Stones—he was still in the Faces, after all—so the Stones decamped to Musicland Studios in Munich in 1974 (where they had cut most of *It's Only Rock 'n Roll*), and later Rotterdam, to check out a handful of potential new guitarists before breaking to do their 1975 Tour of the Americas with Ronnie on guitar, and finally finishing the new record in New York City over a year later.

Black and Blue was less of a follow-up to *It's Only Rock 'n Roll* than it was the results of their quest to find a replacement for Mick Taylor, who foolishly thought there were greener pastures than the Rolling Stones. But despite its rap as the "audition" album with an emphasis on jamming, it is actually the most underrated album (with the possible exception of *Emotional Rescue*) in the Stones catalogue.

Ronnie Wood obviously got the nod, although it's hard to

imagine that there was ever any question, so many are called, so few chosen and all that. Among the potentials that drifted through the studio to play with the Stones were Steve Marriott, Peter Frampton, Harvey Mandel, and Wayne Perkins, the latter two of whom played exceptionally well and made it on to the record, even if they didn't get the gig. Jeff Beck stopped by to jam and whined that "in two hours I got to play three chords—I need a little more energy than that," the kind of thing you'd never hear Keith mutter. Or Robert Johnson, for that matter. Personally, I was rooting for Johnny Thunders—no one bothered to invite him, but just think what a party *that* would have been.

Ronnie is only on a few songs on *Black and Blue*, but most importantly he understood innately the Ancient Art of Weaving, and immediately coalesced around the re-energized core of Charlie and Keith—even Bill sounded back on form—and helped deliver a couple of vicious riff-bashers ("Hey Negrita," "Crazy Mama") and an extremely wobbly cover of Eric Donaldson's reggae classic "Cherry Oh Baby." Meanwhile, Mick and Keith were back to writing genuinely beautiful and badass songs ("Memory Motel," "Hand of Fate") and the Stones ended up sounding not so much like a band trying to follow up past successes as they do a veteran band of assassins just playing at being themselves, and, for the first time since *Exile*, they sounded like they were enjoying their work.

One thing about Ronnie Wood: he seemed destined to be a Rolling Stone. Like Ronald Reagan and Elvis Presley and a few others, Ron Wood was born under his own star, and once he got started, for better or worse, there was no stopping his ascent.

It was meant to be. You could feel it. At the time it all seemed casual enough, but that's obviously the way the Creator designed it. On the Fifth Day, Mick Taylor, and on the Sixth Day, Ronnie Wood, and all of that magick—you wouldn't have trusted any of it if it happened all at once, it wouldn't have been a good story. Nothing good ever happens overnight. Creating worlds takes time.

Brian Jones was essential to the forming of the beast: they needed Brian to conjure the hoodoo of Muddy and Wolf and Bo and Chuck, their spirit animals. Mick Taylor was a surgeon, a specialist brought in to cut closer to the bone. They needed him to slash through the end of the sixties and realign the corps—the Ancient Art of Weaving with Brian had run its course. Taylor was brought in for the Ancient Art of Murder.

It was a short, sharp shot with Mick Taylor, just a couple of tracks on *Let It Bleed* and then his extraordinary knife-wielding on *Exile* and *Sticky Fingers*, really just those two records before they reached the point of diminishing returns with *Goats Head Soup* and *It's Only Rock 'n Roll*. But it was enough. He did his job well, using his guitar like a No. 10 scalpel before being blinded by the lights.

I always wonder, what was the voice in Mick Taylor's head that told him he should quit? *Was it angel or demon?* Because he certainly got fucked on the deal. Any plans he had to be a big star in his own right faded right there, like the last rose of summer.

Charlie fell right in with the new guitar pairing, becoming a bigger part of the cosmic loom. "What was good with Brian is what's good about Ronnie," Charlie noted, "except I think Ronnie is better at it." You could hear the two guitars becoming a blur on the live record, *Love You Live*, compiled from their first tours with Ronnie, the tours of "the Americas" and Europe in 1975 and 1976, plus a side of blues covers recorded in 1977.

Everything you needed to know about rock'n'roll drumming was now on two convenient long-playing phonograph records.

You should play along with them. Seriously, give it a go. Why not? The songs may seem simple enough—but that's because you don't share Charlie's charisma or imagination. There is no way to anticipate his flare, his flourish of magical colors. In his hands, simple songs become labyrinths of soul, each one a new adventure in rhythm. It's impossible to tell where the roll ends and the rock begins, the history of swing fueling a mess of glammed-up gospel and dirty blues. Like a true virtuoso, he sounds effortless and fluid. Like a true jazzer, he's probably making half of it up as he goes along. His hi-hat and snare-drum patterns had become minefields of ingenuity.[4]

The Stones' horn section was gone, old-school R&B was being replaced by a new kind of funk: Billy Preston, whose Afro took up half the stage, had joined the fray on keyboards, and for some reason was allowed to bring his percussion player, Ollie Brown. Billy had a tendency to overplay, and on at least one occasion Keith had to show him his flick-knife[5] and remind him whose band it

---

4 Highly recommended is the official Stones video document, *From the Vault: L.A. Forum—(Live in 1975)*. Ronnie's still just a hired hand, but it's very obvious that this is where he belongs.

5 Keith was almost always armed, a habit he fell into on an early Stones American tour, but he was sensible about it: "The blade should be used for play time only, the shooter to make sure you get your point across."

was—but the doldrums of the last two studio records had been replaced by sheer exuberance.

It probably didn't hurt that Ronnie and Keith were running on pure, pharmaceutical Merck cocaine—one song, one line, a reasonable dose for an adult Rolling Stone—and if you ever wondered the difference between the Rolling Stones' cocaine and the kind of dust everyone else was snarfling in 1975, it was like the difference between watching a porno and being kidnapped by the Army Corps of Engineers—that is, if the Army Corps of Engineers were a team of nymphomaniac Scandinavian flight attendants. Once again, this was the Stones being so of their times as to practically define them. You could practically *hear* the cocaine!

Suddenly everything seemed larger than everything else. The arenas they were playing didn't get any bigger, but the show was *enormous*, and included a giant inflatable penis that Mick, dressed like a spritely Ninja in fierce blue eye-shadow, would climb with various degrees of success. The stage itself was designed to open up somewhat vaginally, like a giant lotus petal.

It was Charlie's idea, the stage design[6]—you can take the boy out of art school and all that—and, anyway, it was their way of competing with the blizzard of arena acts who had all gone in for the trappings of the spectacle and were beginning to hog

---

6 You can decide for yourself if this matters or not, but it's nice to see that everyone listens to Charlie. A lot of drummers don't get that sort of courtesy. He'd continue to contribute to the set designs, working with Mick and a host of designers, lighting guys, etc., for the rest of their career, even as the stages became more like enormous spaceships.

the spotlight: KISS, Bowie, Elton, and their own slew of shitty imitators who needed to be taught that there was no besting the Stones at this game.

The tempos were up, and the attitude was again one of clear rock'n'roll superiority, even as the dance music was moving in— "Hot Stuff" and "Fingerprint File" were a signal shift from the South Side of Chicago to the discotheques of Paris and London and Munich.

Ronnie and Keith quickly became their own circus, their own riot, their own druggy petting zoo. There was a palpable giddiness to the whole affair. Mick, too, realized Ronnie could be a great foil— unlike the last guy, he didn't mind being molested by the singer, why, he was up for anything! Most importantly, with two simpatico guitar players playing as one, the Stones machine had become a unified front, an incomparable din of rhythm and spectacle.

As on the last few tours, with the exception of "Satisfaction," they largely eschewed the pre-1968 stuff—the Brian-era pop songs were like the artifacts of a time when Beatles roamed the earth— but this year they brought back "Get Off of My Cloud" with fresh-cooked cockiness and post-adolescent insouciance, the drum lick reporting loud and clear across the arena. It was a rediscovery of their trace elements. They were mean.

And jazzbo Charlie was the anchor in all of this mayhem. His snare drum, mystically, seemed to have gained power. Guitar amplifiers were getting bigger and bigger, sound systems were taking over like nuclear weapons in a blossoming arms race, smoke machines and laser light shows had become standard operating equipment, drum sets had become the size of furniture showrooms, but Charlie's tiny jazz drum set stayed the same, and he attacked it with a relaxed mastery. The guy who aspired to play in Charlie Parker's combo was now going toe-to-toe with the monster drummers in Led Zeppelin and the Who—and their oversized drum kits—slaying dragons without compromise.

Keith was no longer playing Chuck Berry riffs, he was playing Keith Richards riffs, or, more likely, they were playing him—it was impossible to tell where the man ended and the music began. And so it was with all of them, except Mick, of course, who was always too self-conscious to completely lose himself inside the music.

The development of the wireless microphone certainly didn't help. This was the beginning of the era of the free-range singer, where at any given time he might be a football field's length away from the band, and you can bet it wasn't doing much for his singing, or fanning the flames of intimacy with the band, running around like a sailor on leave, but it was good showbiz.[7] Audiences went nuts for that shit.

"Tumbling Dice" suffered the most from Mick's leaping about. Sometimes he really just needed to settle down and throw strikes—you can't deliver a song about cheating women and low-down gamblers when you are leaping about like a high-school cheerleader. "You Can't Always Get" unwound into an unfortunately long Ronnie Wood guitar solo, the kind of set-stretcher that gave arena

---

7 Much to the credit of Mick and Keith, producing again as "The Glimmer Twins," when they overdubbed the vocals on the record, they worked hard to make them sound crappy and rough—authentic, *sans* the gymnastics.

rock a bad name, but just when you were about to make a trip to the loo, *those drums!* A bump and grind, a combination *shwoop* and tackle—every little snare-drum blast and hi-hat trick was a slippery-when-wet bit of strip-joint tease. This is not the same Charlie Watts who played on "Satisfaction," this is a fully formed jazz magician driving THE GREATEST ROCK'N'ROLL BAND IN THE WORLD, working at extreme volume on a drum kit more suited to a basement speakeasy than a football stadium, and it has to rate as some sort of evolutionary miracle, something along the lines of tadpoles climbing out of the swamp, learning to walk erect, and then learning how to build rockets and bombs.

Most importantly—and nothing was more important—*nothing!*—when Keith started chomping at the opening riff of "Jumpin' Jack Flash," the earth seemed to wobble on its axis, in perfect sympathy with the Rolling Stones' rhythm section. The actual words to the song had become less important than Mick's siren wail: it was no longer about a crossfire hurricane, it actually was one.

Near the end of *Love You Live*, a couple of cherry bombs explode, illicit pyrotechnics set off by enthusiastic fans who valued their fingers less than they did a cheap thrill. It sounded good. Fucking loud. It was exciting. There were no politics to any of this. This was the moment the revolution became entertainment.

EIGHT

RESPECTABLE

THE GREAT GENIUS OF DISCO MUSIC is that it is all about the heartbeat, steady and throbbing. It's easy to relate to the rhythm— you are already living it.

Most disco songs are just slightly quicker than the average resting heartbeat of a moderately excited adult human, enough for a thrill, but without actually being threatening, like that demonic *rock* music. Listening to disco actually raised your pulse beat and gave you a cheap rush, but it didn't kill you, either, which is why disco was so popular at bar mitzvahs as well as in actual discotheques: because it was the perfect tempo for dancing, doing drugs, and fucking all night long, but Grandma could do the Hustle with little chance of falling over dead.

The perfect disco tempo is like a brisk walk—say, the way people walk down the street in Brooklyn, New York, eating pizza, two slices at a time, as seen in the film *Saturday Night Fever*, which was as much a catalyst for the late 1970s mainstream disco boom as anything else.

I say *mainstream* because this was the introduction for a lot of people to disco culture—John Travolta and the Bee Gees and the film's bestselling soundtrack album. It was fucking ubiquitous in 1977, there was no escaping it.

What a lot of people have forgotten is that disco had as much to do with fashion as it did with music, so no wonder they found themselves at cross purposes with the kind of rock fans whose idea of a good time was to see Molly Hatchet or the Outlaws or Foreigner or what was left of Black Sabbath in a hockey arena, where the popular fashion was a worn concert jersey and faded blue jeans. These were the people who brought the cherry bombs to the shows. They were animals! And not that their ranks were rife with philosophy majors, but they sure seemed hip to the transcendentalist ethos, *Beware all enterprises that require new clothes.*

And so the "Disco Sucks" movement, such as it was, blossomed like a bad case of eczema.

Much has been written about the whole blot, with a lot of earnest vitriol accusing white rock fans who couldn't accept a challenge to their own monoculture of being homophobic and racist, and defended by same white dudes calling bullshit: they hated disco because they couldn't find a white three-piece suit that fit their beer-bellied, Shmoo bodies, and, anyway, why all of a sudden did they have to give up the very essence of their identity as fun-loving lunks who loved guitar rock to worship a polyester calf? Most of the Midwestern, hard-rocking Bob Seger fans who hated disco weren't sophisticated enough to know that disco even had Latino and gay and African-American roots. America is a big country, and out in suburbia you got the shopping-mall version.

No one I knew didn't like the Village People because they were presumed to be gay, mostly everyone I knew (a) liked them because the only two songs anyone ever heard by them were funny and catchy enough, or (b) they were completely indifferent or dismissive, because it was just a bunch of guys playing dress-up and dancing to prerecorded music. Ultimately, they were just a harmless novelty act, not as cool as the Banana Splits had been, but then you can never really have it all, at least not all at once. The fact that they were gay icons wasn't a thing in suburbia, a place where jocks went to football stadiums to see a band called Queen.

Anyway, it was clearly all in the name of good fun. It was just pop music, not a lifestyle commitment—*that's* when things got dicey. Disco Dans fetishized polyester shirts and slacks (slacks!) and gold chains, expensive haircuts, white suits, and high-powered cologne.

I remember my mom taking me for a haircut when I was thirteen or so, at the height of this madness, and when she saw the trendy, feathered sweep the so-called barber had sculpted out of what had been a perfectly good head of hair, she was delighted that I looked so cool (which made her, by extension, a cool mom), and I just cried my fucking eyes out, mortified that my very soul had been stolen from me, and wore a ski cap for the next two months, even though it was the middle of July. I loved the O'Jays and Donna Summer and KC and the Sunshine Band as much as the next guy. The Jackson 5 never went out of style. We played those records at parties, along with the latest from Elton John, Stevie Wonder, and whatever other else was popular on the radio that week—that's how guys got to dance with girls. That's how many of my best and worst ideas were formed.

I watched *Soul Train* religiously (for the music) and *Solid Gold* occasionally (for the dancers), but I wasn't buying into this plastic-fantastic fashion bullshit, and after that haircut I didn't even let her buy me new jeans for fear that they'd do weird things to my ass.

Very few people I know went out and got disco makeovers, and those that did were positively despotic in their ready-to-wear identities, as any working-class, dyed-in-the-wool rock fan was who clung to his favorite concert T-shirt like a red badge of courage. And now there was a war, disco vs. rock—whatever hippie hangover was still simmering in the late 1970s, namely prog-rock and longhair boogie bands, there was a new urban theosophy that disco was going to be the neutron bomb to put an end to it all. It was a very aggressive pose. And naturally *everyone* hated the punk-rockers, who were the real freaks. It would be a while before anyone realized it was all the same shit.

Meanwhile, the big secret was that discotheques were safe spaces for rich people. That's why there were so many aging celebrities there—it was approved decadence. Disco was mama's heartbeat for insecure adults. It was a chance for a little bit of excitement without completely losing control. It was very repetitive. It was comforting. Discotheques were like giant wombs, if wombs had spinning silver balls and DJ booths in them.

Sometimes the beats were a little faster, if you were doing coke, sometimes a little slower, if you were doing 'ludes, but there it was: *a sex beat*, and as much as the great dance mixes were perfected in a glorious gay underground, it translated to suburbia with shocking ease. Even crud like "A Fifth of Beethoven" was tolerated, because it had a good hook. That beat was just enough of a rush for the squares—your gay cousin could dig it, but so could your parents, who felt hip doing the Bump. It was urbane with an edge, and it was on sale at the shopping mall. Suburban chicks loved it—anything to get their Led Zeppelin–lovin' boyfriends out of their T-shirts and torn jeans. Unlike rock, at least disco smelled nice.

The real reason disco sucked was "Disco Duck." How could an entire cultural movement be taken seriously when a song like "Disco Duck" could become a legitimate hit? Not that rock wasn't stupid, but it took a lot longer to get there.

After *Saturday Night Fever*—and everyone I knew loved it, no matter how many Jethro Tull albums they had piled up next to their bong—came a slew of self-parody and idiocy that just ate itself. Oddly, a lot of it took place on roller skates.

The *Playboy's Roller Disco and Pajama Party* television special (1979)—which was even dumber than it sounds—was the straw in the camel's back. When Hugh Hefner, Mr. Playboy, jumped on the bandwagon with this juvenelic act of desperation to remain relevant, the dream was over.[1] It was like Disco Altamont.

And yet the most horrifying trend of the times wasn't the increasingly lame disco records that were being stamped out without any of the soul or quality production or actual songwriting of the first great wave—it was a long run from "Love Train" to "Macho Man"—it was the establishment rock bands of the time being told by their record companies that they needed to get on the disco bandwagon if they wanted to move units, and these dinosaurs, living in fear of extinction, actually went along with it. We had come a long way indeed since Elvis and Little Richard and the championship power of the individual.

And so we got rocker Rod Stewart plodding along with "Da Ya Think I'm Sexy?"; the Kinks, who got their start as proto-punk British Invasion upstarts before becoming ponderous, Beatles-influenced art rockers, were now having a go at the disco thing with "(I Wish I Could Fly Like) Superman"; craven hard-rockers KISS proved once and for all that they had zero shame and even less scruples with "I Was Made for Lovin' You"; and even countrified cokeheads and cosmic cowboys like the Eagles and the Grateful Dead each took a stab at the spinning mirror ball with "One of These Nights" and "Shakedown Street," one of the few disco songs designed primarily for pot heads. Paul McCartney, famously of the Beatles, thumped along aimlessly with "Goodnight Tonight."[2] Even antiques like Paul Anka and

1 Juvenelic = juvenile + imbecilic.

2 It would be dishonest not to mention that all of these songs were hits.

Frankie Avalon had a go at it. But perhaps most embarrassingly of all, even smarty-pants prog-rockers Pink Floyd managed to glue a disco beat onto their contrived dystopian light show to score a No. 1 hit. When it came to rock'n'roll, *hoo boy*, the culture had really shit the bed.

So how did the Rolling Stones, THE GREATEST ROCK'N'ROLL BAND IN THE WORLD, snake by with their disco bid, "Miss You," the first song on their monstrously popular *Some Girls* record, in the summer of 1978?

Well, for one, they were really good at it. They made disco sound *greasy* and *wet*.

Mick and Charlie, at least, were long-time fans. They weren't Johnny-come-latelies to club music—they had been trolling international dance floors for years, Mick making the scene and boosting riffs for the next Stones record, and Charlie just digging the music. Mr. Jazz was no moldy fig—he may have been in a lifelong romance with Charlie Parker, but that didn't mean he couldn't hear what was happening around him, and he fell in love with the Philadelphia sound when it was exploding in the early 1970s, especially the mighty *shwoop* of its first great drummer, Earl Young, who seemed to be on every hip dance record for a while there, from the Intruders' "(Win, Place or Show) She's a Winner" to the O'Jays' "Love Train" and "Back Stabbers," to Harold Melvin & the Blue Notes' "The Love I Lost," not to mention tons of stuff with the Trammps, including "Disco Inferno," plus sessions with the Spinners, the Stylistics, MFSB, and dozens more.[3]

By 1978, the Rolling Stones (unlike the Kinks, *et al.*) didn't have to be told by some turd in a suit that they needed a disco beat to stay relevant—all you had to do was go back one record, to *Black and Blue*, and the very first song, "Hot Stuff," which was what Jagger even then called "a disco departure," or two years

---

3 One odd thing about Charlie's listening habits, which are by far the widest and most eclectic of this lot: unlike Keith, who can be pretty hardcore when it comes to blues and R&B and rock'n'roll and reggae and roots, Charlie was all over the place, extremely open not just to old-time jazz *à la* Louis Armstrong and the big bands and the jazz codgers he is always cooing about, but obviously his hero, Charlie Parker, whose advanced concepts of harmony and melody and velocity genuinely *frightened* the old timers (and still turn off a lot of self-impressed, self-described jazz fans who can't get past Miles Davis's more mellow outings—seriously, have you tried listening to Charlie Parker lately?), but also to the bent modernism of Ornette Coleman and explorations of John Coltrane, and the atonal, free-form pyrotechnics of pianist Cecil Taylor, all of which he says are very easy for him to listen to—putting him in a distinct minority of intellectual weirdoes—not to mention his love for disco, dance music, and the occasional modern rock band. It was his support, along with Mick's, in fact, that got Prince on to a couple of shows with the Stones in 1981. Charlie and Mick were nuts for him—Keith wasn't with it, but his bandmates ruled the day, and Prince got the opening slot before the decidedly more middle-of-the-road, MTV-friendly George Thorogood, and the J. Geils Band. Sadly for Prince, the audience didn't share Charlie and Mick's enthusiasm, and dressed in black panties and thigh-high boots, he was soundly booed off the stage under a shower of food and beer. No doubt the same assholes who booed him then are bragging about seeing him now.

before, to the dance-floor stylings of "Fingerprint File" on *It's Only Rock 'n Roll*. Anyone who was paying attention already knew that their ever-expanding concept of R&B was wide enough to have given an ill-advised amount of real estate to both of those songs on *Love You Live*, space that could have just as easily been given over to solid rock'n'roll senders like "All Down the Line" or "Rip This Joint"—songs the Stones made their reputation with, cutting throats with them on the previous tour—but that was a battle that Keith lost in the mixing room. There ain't no stopping progress, I suppose.

So when the Stones cut "Miss You," as much as it was obviously another grand Mick idea to stay *au courant* (it took Keith some convincing, but ultimately he saw the wisdom in Mick's madness), you can't say they were selling out—they had been playing great black dance music for years, and had just changed the beat with the times. They had a bad track record for chasing trends, but when they got it right, they owned it.

As it turned out, they were an incredibly good disco band—or, more likely, an incredibly swank rock'n'roll band who could give it up and turn it loose.[4] Would Mick Jagger have ever become such a great dancer if he didn't have such a great band behind him?

Charlie's drumming was impeccable—disciplined and unadorned. He used the *shwoop*, like Al Jackson, with surgical discretion, its overuse having become the hallmark of wedding-

---

4 For anyone not paying attention, aside from "Miss You," their other great disco numbers include "Everything Is Turning to Gold," "Dance" (Pts. 1 and II), and "Emotional Rescue," all of them excellent.

band drummers trying to keep up with the disco times. In Charlie's hands, it *swung*. Even playing disco, there was that slight wobble, keeping the beat just behind Keith. He pushed the song forward with *urgency*. And he was shrewd—he hadn't played this minimally since the Brian Jones days. As ever, this was Why Charlie Watts Matters: there was the *anticipation* in the groove, and the *penetration* was left, as it should be, to whatever happened after closing time.

It sounded like the Rolling Stones, doing that thing they do—as it turned out, the Ancient Art of Weaving had its place in disco. "Miss You" was a minor masterpiece—it was just one big hook, with a shit ton of New York City thrown on top, including a nice bit of blues harp, just in case you were wondering with whom you were dealing.

Cranky rockists may have pooh-poohed it, but just for a second, because *Some Girls* wasn't dominated by *disco songs*, it was a gorgeous mess of *Rolling Stones songs*, and "Miss You" was just one of them. At the same time they were laying claim to the dance floor, they were also proving themselves a great punk-rock band, and a top-tier country band that dabbled in jazz and torch songs.

Actually, for a gang that had been copping Marvin Gaye and gigging with Stevie Wonder, not to mention lashing out with "Street Fighting Man" and "Happy" for years, they were uniquely suited to play disco *and* punk—they had been at it for years, they just called it something else.

∘ ∘ ∘

In 1977, when they got to the Pathé-Marconi studio in Paris to begin work on *Some Girls*, the Stones were a band on a mission— no more resting on their laurels as THE GREATEST ROCK'N'ROLL BAND IN THE WORLD, no more participation trophies, that shit had to be won on the field. Keith Richards was facing a life in stir thanks to his heroin bust in Toronto, and this could be the last time.

Did I forget to mention Keith's heroin bust? Dang.

So here's the short of it: At the end of the 1975–1976 tours that became *Love You Live*, the Stones had the idea to play a small club, the El Mocambo, in Toronto, and focus on some of the old blues numbers they cut their teeth on. Unfortunately, upon arrival, the locale *gendarme* snagged Keith's girlfriend Anita Pallenberg with a dirty spoon and soon enough found Keith's stash, enough smack for a junkie wedding party—although in my book, a room full of passed-out people, no matter how good-looking they are, just isn't my idea of a good time. But each to his own. I don't judge.[5]

At any rate, somehow they made the gig a few days later and cut an old Chuck Berry favorite, a Muddy Waters number, and a remarkable—for Charlie's spectacular, calypso-style drumming— version of Bo Diddley's "Crackin' Up," but don't be fooled, because

---

5 For the firsthand account, again, once again, read Keith's most excellent book, *Life*. So few people can make heroin sound so charming. Incidentally, it took a team of Canadian Mounties and the horses they rode in to wake Keith up at his hotel before they busted him. Apparently, this is an example of proper Canadian etiquette—they really are quite nice, those Canadians—they are not allowed to arrest anyone who isn't conscious.

most of it was overdubbed later, which happens a lot more than you might imagine, even if you imagine that it happens a lot.

And this is how we get to *Some Girls*.

The surprising thing is how energized they were in 1978—some people might have reacted differently to the odds of a long stretch in the Canadian hoosegow, but they also had the times biting them on the ass, which was a great motivator. Disco might have been all the rage, but punk rock was charging straight up their collective bum, basically threatening to eat them from the inside out. That the Rolling Stones needed to own the end of the 1970s was less of a choice than an imperative, a last gasp for relevancy.

And so "Miss You," the first song on the record, was a full-tilt disco explosion, but it was followed by "When the Whip Comes Down," the most exuberant song they had cut in years, which twanged like a wire fence but was decidedly punk rock by any rock-dork standards, and it wasn't even the most exuberant number on the album. They were just getting started, and if any idiotic Ted Nugent fans still had their feathers ruffled because they thought *disco* was *queer*, well, the joke was on them, because "When the Whip Comes Down" was a first-person account of Mick Jagger working as a gay hustler—"*I was gay in New York, just a fag in L.A.*"—but it rocked, insistently and authoritatively, and laid down the gauntlet for any punks still sniggering at the old men, setting the pace for the toughest and sleaziest record the Rolling Stones would ever make, which was no little feat.

The Stones didn't understand punk rock, not in so much as they were sitting around listening to the Sex Pistols or the Ramones or the Damned. There was a generation gap, to be sure, and an economic one, as well. It was one thing to pal around dance clubs in Munich or Studio 54 in New York with other well-heeled celebrity cokeheads, but punk rock was a youth movement, highly politically motivated by the working class in Britain, if not so much in the US, where it always was as much an art statement as a political uprising. But it was never about *having* money, it was always about having *none*, and not the kind of thing entrenched millionaires were ever going to fully understand, no matter the quality of the music. After all, the *raison d'être* of the Sex Pistols was to put the last wave of bloated old rotters who had lost contact with their audiences out of business. Whatever limited future the Pistols had, they were building it on the ash heap of the aristocracy, and that included the Rolling Stones.

A funny thing—while the Stones were plotting their response to this youthquake, their would-be rivals, the Clash, were recording reggae and rock'n'roll of very high standards, along with this so-called punk-rock music, and getting ready to tour the States with their personally invited guest, Bo Diddley. Sadly, Clash fans often had trouble understanding the mash-up of rock'n'roll cultures.[6] They hadn't figured it out yet, that it was all the same shit.

6 It should be mentioned that this was before the Who invited the Clash on to their stage—this was still that dark time when "punk" was the enemy of "classic rock," as much as disco had been, even though all the "Disco Sucks" morons were somehow finding lame excuses to accept such bullshit from Pink Floyd, the Kinks, etc., etc. A more ironic moment would come later, when the Ramones and the Sex Pistols and the Clash were all suddenly considered "classic rock," as if none of this had ever happened.

As for the Stones, their *contretemps* with the upstarts seemed distant at best—it was obvious they were *aware*, but they weren't really *tuned-in*. They spoke halfheartedly about an appreciation of the energy, an acknowledgment that punk rock wasn't that much different than what they had done once upon a time—but never without a stern dismissal that these punks couldn't play, or some inane comment about all that spitting, the kind of thing they likely saw on the telly and assumed it represented an entire artistic movement, as jaded adults so often do. The good thing is that, instead of just screaming for the kids to get off of their lawn, the Stones got out the big guns and opened fire.

∘ ∘ ∘

The Stones got it. The Beatles got it. Ray Charles and Chuck Berry got it. But some folks just don't understand country music. Take, for example, musical bigot Buddy Rich, the world's most celebrated drum virtuoso, the kind of musical know-it-all who really doesn't know what he is talking about, but also *really doesn't know what he's talking about*.

Bloviating to big-band-singer-turned-hepcat talk-show host Mike Douglas in 1973—who co-hosted his show with folks as diverse as Barbra Streisand, Sly Stone, and John and Yoko[7]—THE WORLD'S GREATEST DRUMMER shared his opinion about America's "biggest music":

"It's about time that this country grew up in its musical taste

7 The Rolling Stones were his guests in 1964, when it was still largely a local show out of Cleveland. He was much nicer to them than Dean Martin was.

rather than making the giant step backwards that country music is doing ... it is so simple that anybody can sing it, anybody can do it, anyone can play it on one string."

He went on to proselytize abut jazz, modestly inserting himself in a group that included Miles Davis, Charlie Parker, and Art Tatum, before picking up the thread: "I don't think you have to create too much, man, to be a hillbilly ... [audience audibly uncomfortable] ... anybody can sing *wah wah wah* ..."

And here comes our host, who's heard enough. "Music makes people happy in different ways," he offers, diplomatically.

Buddy was having no part of it. Diplomacy was never his bag. "If I'm going to sit and listen to you sing and I'm going to listen to Frank [Sinatra] or Tony Bennett, there is enough emotion there to carry me through whatever period I'm going through, but if I have to listen to *Glen Campbell* ..." He feigns the look of someone who just drank some bad milk and is about to vomit, before comparing country music to pornography, which probably did a lot more to sell Conway Twitty records than the crappy old Buddy Rich Big Band cassettes he peddled at his gigs.

Anyway, when I say he *really* didn't know what he was taking about, I mean that his buddy, *jazz* singer Tony Bennett, had a No. 1 hit with a Hank Williams song, "Cold, Cold Heart," and he even performed it at the Grand Ole Opry—quite the honor in some circles, I understand.

His pal Frank Sinatra recorded songs by Eddy Arnold and John Denver, not to mention a great duet of Bobbie Gentry's "Ode to Billie Joe" with noted hillbilly chanteuse Ella Fitzgerald, and (gasp!)

a very easygoing turn on Glen Campbell's "Gentle on My Mind" (also covered by stick-in-the-mud Dean Martin, Andy Williams, Aretha Franklin, and Bing Crosby, to name but a few)—all great songs with little room for the drummer to "just wail," as Mr. Rich has generally encouraged. Oh, and then there was the genius of soul, Ray Charles, who recorded two volumes worth of *Modern Sounds in Country and Western Music*, both smasheroos.

Anyway, back to the Rolling Stones, who had always loved country music, and played it at an unheard-of level: the sleaze of "Let It Bleed" and "Torn and Frayed," the impossible shuffle of "Sweet Virginia," the lithe touch of "No Expectations," "Dear Doctor," or "Factory Girl," the beautifully druggy laments of "Wild Horses" and "Sister Morphine." Their most famous country songs, "Honky Tonk Women" and "Dead Flowers," were cheap pastiche by comparison.

On *Some Girls*, the Stones had found a powerful new approach to country music: they stomped the living shit out of it and called it "punk."

° ° °

Buddy Rich might have died a lot happier had he opened up his heart, for in country music, there is *salvation*.[8]

---

8 After an amazing career as America's most famous big band drummer, working with everyone from Tommy Dorsey to Louis Armstrong and Ella Fitzgerald, Buddy Rich finished his career playing with groups stocked largely with college students and talented amateurs sporting poorly printed Buddy Rich polo shirts, working community colleges and high schools. His obit in the *L.A. Times* reported that

Which isn't to say there aren't plenty of crappy country records—in fact it is highly likely that the majority of them suck. Same could be said for disco, or heavy metal, rock, whatever. There's tons of bad poetry, too, but that doesn't mean I'm throwing Allen Ginsberg out with the bathwater. And, not incidentally, if you really feel like breaking it down, give Zeppelin a fresh listen and you'll hear more genuinely badass twang in Jimmy Page's guitar playing—James Burton, Joe Maphis, Scotty Moore, Cliff Gallup, etc.—than in most modern country music.

So what have we learned? I mean, besides the fact that Buddy Rich was a snob? It really must have been a drag, having that much talent.

The great country drummers have touched more lives than Buddy Rich and a thousand other so-called drumming virtuosos. Country music endures: Jimmy Van Eaton, the Sun Records house drummer who played with everyone from Jerry Lee Lewis (who called him "the creative rock'n'roll drummer") to Roy Orbison, and Bob Dylan favorite Billy Riley and his Little Green Men, was as much of a pioneer of rock'n'roll as the cats from Chicago and New Orleans. Naturally he started out as a jazz drummer, because,

---

on his deathbed, a nurse asked him if he were allergic to anything, to which he replied, "Yes, country and western music." He was also quoted as saying, "If you don't have ability, you wind up playing in a rock band." He was famous for getting into fistfights in parking lots and losing his temper when he ran out of reefer. Dusty Springfield once slapped the toupee off his head when they were sharing a bill in the late '60s, after he called her a "fucking broad." The bootleg recordings of him screaming at his band after gigs are legendary. They are available on an internet near you.

after all, that's how this whole floating crap game got going in the first place.

W. S. Holland was the guy who put the train rhythm behind Johnny Cash on "Folsom Prison Blues," "Ring of Fire," and "I Walk the Line," not to mention playing on Carl Perkins's "Blue Suede Shoes," "Honey Don't," and "Matchbox" (all covered by the Beatles), and even if he's not a household name, you can bet more people have positive memories of his music—*that cool train rhythm!*—than anything Buddy Rich has ever touched.[9]

And then there was Charlie Watts. And this is just one more reason Why Charlie Watts Matters: because when it came to country, disco, blues, punk, whatever, this guy could swing a *battleship*.

Charlie never played better than he did on *Some Girls*. There was more imagination and precision in his playing than ever

---

9 Country drummers were as tough as they came, and not the kind of cats you want to be calling out on national TV: Paul English, Willie Nelson's drummer for fifty-plus years, was a hoodlum, pimp, and "police character" first, and a drummer second. He never left home without his piece. He'd been in an actual gunfight with Willie, fighting off angry family members with a shotgun; legendarily used the motivation of his pistol to get paid by lowlife promoters countless times; and kept everyone on the road *honest* long before it became one big happy family—it has been said that if you "mess with Willie Nelson, the next thing you'll see is the wrong end of a gun held by the devil himself." That would be Paul English. And then there was Tarp Tarrant, Jerry Lee Lewis's frantic drummer for over a dozen years—you can hear him on the aptly titled 1964 LP *The Greatest Live Show on Earth*—who lost his job when he was arrested for armed robbery. I have no doubt that either of them would have been only too happy to put a slug in Buddy Rich if they had heard his anti-country yapping.

before. Every song was a fresh take on the art of rock'n'roll drumming.

"Charlie is so magnificent you expect him to go on getting better," Keith told *Melody Maker* shortly after they completed *Some Girls*, "and if he doesn't get better at a session, you sorta moan at him, 'Why aren't you better than last time, 'cos you always are!'"

Also, Charlie Watts was never called an asshole.

o o o

Some Girls was the Stones' redemption. Gone was the sonic murk that weighed down *Goats Head Soup* and *It's Only Rock 'n Roll*—was it just me, or did those records sound like the needle on my turntable needed to be replaced? The so-called punk songs on *Some Girls* twanged with clarity and Telecaster thump, a lot of which had to do with engineer Chris Kimsey's recording techniques and a fresh set of MESA/Boogie amps. Even the bass stung with a crispness that had not been heard on a Stones record before.

You could really hear it on the later tours, when they slowed down a bit: those songs were pure outlaw country. "When the Whip Comes Down" and "Respectable" were proof that Keith and Charlie—and now Ronnie—attacking Chuck Berry riffs with the feverish life-or-death drive of a posse fighting off the zombie apocalypse was the most compelling force in rock'n'roll, especially with Mick revisiting popular themes like selling his body and doing drugs with the president. They hit those songs with string-bending

Tough, tough, tough, tough, tough, tough: disco meets punk, 1978. (Photofest)

angst and countrified finesse, a hybrid of fresh-fanged attitude and old-time rock'n'roll. A notch less willfully perverse and "Respectable," especially, would have been the perfect song for Merle or Willie or Kris or Waylon. As it was, *Some Girls* was a redefinition of terms, and a new claim to show-business authority—a fresh warning that anyone else in the same racket might want to seriously reconsider just what the fuck they were doing.

Everything was stripped down and sounded like it was recorded live on the floor, no tricks, by a band that had become the darlings of the discotheque and the poster boys for establishment rock but could still hold their own in a bar fight.

The Stones' idea of punk obviously came from within. Whereas Mick lifted his disco ideas from a night out dancing, the punk-rock songs seemed to be more like what they *thought* punk-rock songs were *supposed* to sound like—fast and shot-through with outrage and attitude—but without the barrage of *barre* chords of the Sex Pistols or the Ramones. That's just not how the Stones played.[10]

It wasn't punk-by-numbers, it was the Rolling Stones, and their music was far closer to the edge of chaos—tempos flying, jazz drums battling to escape the jungle of rock'n'roll fundamentalism—than the Sex Pistols or the Ramones or the Clash, all of whom had excellent but very predictable rhythm sections. The Ramones, especially, had to keep it moving straight ahead, like a well-honed military assault, with no room for improvisation. It was a precision affair, the exact opposite of the Stones: Johnny Ramone promised a band that was "pure white rock'n'roll, with no blues influence." Inflammatory, to be sure, especially from a band that worshipped Phil Spector and '60s girl groups, but he was honest when he said there would be no syncopation: everyone played on the beat—one hint of boogie and they would have been done for—and somehow they made it swing like mad.

The Stones had no such constraints. "Shattered" was the ultimate New York City rock'n'roll song, at least as far as they managed to gleefully capture the vibe of the place, championing a self-destructive mecca for sex and success and singing in

---

10 Actually, as Johnny Rotten has quite correctly said of the Sex Pistols, "We *controlled* the energy—the songs aren't raging fast, they're real slow-tempoed, but they come over *blistering*."

Yiddish, all while sending it up as a maggot-infested rat haven for money-grabbers and fashion victims. But what the fuck was it? It had a sort of a disco beat, but it wasn't *disco-friendly*. It sounded *punk*, but it was layered with pedal steel guitar. And that damn MXR phase-shifter, which was fucking *everywhere* on that record—you'd think they'd have had enough of it after "Beast of Burden."

Speaking of "Beast of Burden," was it a country song or an R&B song? I have no fucking clue. Ditto "Just My Imagination," their third go at a Temptations number, twanged with a snarling edge, a hard slap to the head of what was once a smooth ballad—it sounded forlorn, swampy, and rural, but also streetwise, insistent, and slightly more angry than wistful, as was the Temptations' original. It was an amazing bit of soul music. And, like every other song on *Some Girls*, it was shot through with the Ancient Art of Weaving—whose definition by now must surely include the drums—and a wanton disregard for the concept of finishing any song at the same tempo at which it started.

Seriously, who knew what was what anymore? The title track sounded like a filthy drinking song, all about Chinese girls and black girls and white girls and pretty much every other kind of girl and what they thought they wanted or needed, and there was no protest, no outcry—as reasonable as such outrage may have been—that was going to stop them from carrying on, and certainly not with that drum part, one of the loosest-tightest miracles Charlie had ever conjured. It was a just a dirty toss-off of a song, and yet Charlie was fulfilling every promise he had ever made behind the kit from *Ya-Ya's* onward, every *shwoop*, every off-kilter snare roll, and every crack at his brand new China cymbal.

And this is a big deal, the China cymbal.

It was an oddball piece of hardware, especially so for someone who had been so conservative with his gear. Charlie never went in for gimmicks. For most of his career he stuck to just two cymbals, a ride and a smaller crash cymbal, minimal even among minimalists. The exotic explosion of the China cymbal, what is sometimes called a *trashcan cymbal*, seemed counterintuitive to the basic premise of the Stones sound.

Years ago you would see exotic China cymbals in the cobbled-together kits of early jazzers, as one of their many contraptions: exotic tam-tams and temple blocks, bell trees, bicycle horns, etc. If you have ever heard of a drum set referred to as a "trap set," now you know: it is just shorthand for "contraptions." Years later, the China cymbal was championed by a handful of swing drummers for a bit more drive behind large horn sections. Mel Lewis, the rare big-band drummer known more for his humility and musicality than flash, was a big fan of riding on the China cymbal, which he used to push the horn section without obliterating them. Jake Hanna, another swing-era holdout who powered later versions of Woody Herman's big band, was known to have given Charlie one as a gift.

But by the late 1970s and '80s, it was generally the province of prog-rockers and metal heads of varying degrees of talent who used oversized Chinas mounted upside-down to create a wickedly abrasive *ka-kang* to punch holes in otherwise indistinguishable drum solos, to punctuate dizzying blizzards of double bass drums, and get a cheap pop out of virginal Dungeons & Dragons fans who were thrilled to tears by these sorts of parlor tricks. It was the drumming equivalent of a confetti cannon.

Leave it to Charlie Watts to rediscover the jazz in such a thing. He had experimented with it early on—there are photos of him hanging the China cymbal in the early part of their career—but it would never have worked when they were still wading in the deep end of the pool of R&B traditionalism. But somehow the China cymbal, in all of its noisy glory, found its way on to *Some Girls*, adding a new flavor for the new era of the Stones.

The China cymbal gave the whole proceeding a bit of unexpected, raw, smudged color. There was no denying it was exciting, but just like everything else, it called for discretion. Against convention, Charlie mounted his right side up, in a way it had generally not been played since before the New Deal. "This takes quite a hard bash every night, and they split on the edge... they weren't really made to be played the way I play them," he remarked, when describing his setup for a promo video.

In the context of the Stones, it was a disruptive bit of poetry— it wasn't mellow or pretty in any conventional sense. It had no trace history in Chicago blues or R&B or soul, and yet it fit into the late-1970s Rolling Stones flawlessly. It was sharp and short, and just when you thought Charlie had the market cornered on percussive quirkiness, here comes the trashcan cymbal. It bloomed from a nuanced effect on *Some Girls* to the go-to face-slapper in their live shows, a gentlemanly fuck-you from the jazzbo behind the kit, and fully blossomed into its own phylum of fauna on the nearly flawless follow-up, *Emotional Rescue*: the ragged crash of the China cymbal was as much a part of the hook on the hit "She's So Cold" as was the guitar riff, and it gave the song a perfect ironic sizzle. Every tour, every record that followed, would be peppered with that sound. It was the final length of twine in the Ancient Art of Weaving. Not another rock'n'roll drummer in a million could have pulled it off in the modern era without making it seem like a cheap effect, but in the hands of Mr. Watts, it added true grit to the country-turned-punk, it lit up the R&B and soul, it crackled perfectly across the pop tunes.

The beauty, of course, is that it came so late in their career—and this is one more reason Why Charlie Watts Matters: he made them sound unique, *again*. He was *still evolving*.

In a world of hard-rock arena hacks and bar bands who thought that copping the Stones' sound was mostly an excuse to be sloppy with Chuck Berry and the Jack Daniel's, the China cymbal was like the last petal that needed to bloom, the last flash of flower-power gone wrong that turned an otherwise agreeable spring into a revolution summer. It was the final sparkle of aggression needed to complete this leg of the Rolling Stones' epic journey. Once more, Charlie Watts had brought the blues into the future.

∘ ∘ ∘

By the time they finished recording, Keith was well on his way to being clean, only shooting up *occasionally* in the bathroom during sessions.[11] Looking at seven years in jail often has a salutary effect. Oddly, though, Charlie had begun toying with smack, and Keith had to tell him NO—and thankfully he listened, for a while. It would get messy again later, and we'll get there, but somehow they kept it together for the time being.

The 1978 tour to support the record was everything it possibly should have been: a warning. The live document of the tour, *Some Girls—Live in Texas '78*, is to the Ronnie Wood era what *Ladies and Gentlemen: The Rolling Stones* was for Mick Taylor. Of course, things change, six years is an eternity in this business—technology, fashion, politics, drug habits, even the way people listened to music

---

11 The *Some Girls* sessions were so productive that they churned out an entire, additional album's worth of top-flight country songs, most of which were later polished and released as a bonus disc on a deluxe remastered *Some Girls* package, and are worth every farthing. Twelve killer cuts and not one of them as remotely dumb as the hit "Far Away Eyes." "Do You Think I Really Care" may be the best country song about New York City ever—who else could write a heartbreaker about the D Train and the Long Island expressway?—not to mention a Hank Williams cover, and Keith doing a particularly high-and-lonesome version of Waylon Jennings's signature "We Had It All." "Claudine," a killer rockabilly about the murder of skier Spider Savage by his socialite girlfriend ("*Now I threaten my wife with a gun / But I always leave the safety on*"), and the hard-swinging shuffle "Too Young" ("*I tried to take it easy, put my dick back on a leash … she's so young*") were as low-down and rocking a pair of songs as Mick ever perpetrated, which is saying a mouthful (take that as you will), and never mind Keith going to jail, maybe Mick kept these off the record so he could stay on the street and look after their affairs. It's hard to figure why they didn't just put it out at the time—they could have had another homerun on their hands. Maybe they didn't want their secret known, that the Rolling Stones were THE GREATEST COUNTRY BAND IN THE WORLD.

had all been flipped on their head. But the band emerged unified in seriousness of purpose.

It was the best they'd played since the galvanizing tours of the early 1970s, and they declared their intentions with the conviction of a man nailing his grievances to the church door. They may not have been as heavy as Zep, but those tempos were *up up up up up* …

As ever, Mick went more than one toke over the line, but he wouldn't be Mick if he didn't. Did he really need to change the words of "Sweet Little Sixteen" from "*tight dresses and lipstick*" to "*tight dresses and Tampax*"? Wasn't turning tricks and shooting dope and having sex with slave-girls enough? At least when he sang, "*I don't know where to draw the line,*" in "Starfucker," he was telling the truth, which counts for a lot.

And then there was his T-shirt, a Vivienne Westwood number with a swastika on it under the word "DESTROY." Sadder than thinking that wearing a swastika shirt was cool was that Johnny Rotten had already made it famous in the Sex Pistols. Boosting riffs from Chuck Berry is one thing, buying your punk couture off the rack was a *shanda*.

But everyone was gaga for the new Stones record. Everyone could claim a piece of it—the Stones seemed to have gotten over their rock star selves for a moment, and were reconnecting to their old audience and making new fans all at once. Once again they were the band of the people. When they dug into their guitars, and Charlie breathed magic and venom and joy into every song—shaking stadiums with a set of drums designed to work Harlem nightclubs—it was impossible to deny that they were at the top of their game.

Over the years there had been the slow gestating of the Charlie Watts *style*, now there was the Charlie Watts *sound*. Somehow, adding the China cymbal made him sound even leaner—there was no weight to the thing, no decay, no overtones, no confusing it with a ringing telephone. It was all attack. It was like being slapped by Bruce Lee.

Onstage, "Shattered" was taken at an almost impossible clip, and there was still no telling if it were disco or punk, but it was definitely leaning toward the latter. When Mick barks, "*To live in this town you must be tough tough tough tough tough*," a sentiment echoed with authority by the snare drum, you were getting the idea that these were definitely the wrong guys to fuck with.

"Jumpin' Jack Flash," the perennial closing number, was not just defiant, it had become a *testimonial*—relentless riff-bashing with no regard for tempo, only for blowing the heads off of a stadium full of young people. It was muscular and overly enthusiastic. They hit the stage with no assumptions that their reputation had preceded them, and they came out every night to prove what was rightfully theirs—they were the best goddam rock'n'roll band in the world.

"Love in Vain," a serviceable Robert Johnson cover on *Let It Bleed*, had now become a showstopping piece of drum legislation, an ancient blues renegotiating itself from the inside out. No one else in the world could have tackled it with such perfect audacity and yet kept it authentic. It was old meets new—Mingus meets

Led Zeppelin, although none of the Stones would have agreed. None of them considered Zeppelin subtle enough to be taken entirely seriously.

Even "Miss You" slammed. On the record it was sleazy, lubricated fun. Live, it was an example of what a team of seasoned second-floor men could do with a good riff.

In Memphis, just for fun, they nailed a version of "Hound Dog," and Charlie got to do the D. J. Fontana thing after all of these years. Of course he made it his own, compressing the big triplet bump-and-grind to, well, let's just say he pushed it ever so gingerly from *anticipation* to *penetration*. Discretion is always the better part of valor, and often the better part of valor is knowing when to stick it in.

NINE

HANG FIRE

IT MAY HAVE BEEN THE LONG EXHALE after the triumphalism of the last tour, but the ennui was palpable. The very second the calendar page turned to 1980, everything began to suck.

Well, Keith was free, but the times were changing yet again.[1]

---

1 Keith's penance for his heroin bust was a benefit concert for the Canadian National Institute for the Blind. Nice judges they've got up there in Canada: they figured out that no one was going to benefit from Keith being behind bars, and that everyone would be better off if he got clean and did a charity gig. The show was billed as the New Barbarians—Ron Wood's party-on-wheels pickup band, featuring Keith and a handful of ringers, which hit the road after the Stones' *Some Girls* tour. Their set went over great, but when the Stones showed up to play, it was the spiritual equivalent of a jetliner taking off. They shredded through the best of their '78 set, but the clear highlight was the completely mesmerizing and nearly disastrous version of "Starfucker." I played the first couple of minutes of it over and over again—a bootleg of the show, *Blind Date*, was issued soon afterward. (It's easy to find, you should look it up.) I played it for my friends, who thought I was nuts for championing this mess.

Within the first year of the new decade, John Lennon was dead, Ronald Reagan and Maggie Thatcher were giggling like schoolchildren about wonderful new wars, and the Moral Majority, an exploding AIDS crisis, and MTV—a high-pitched corporate claw-back to co-opt the rock'n'roll revolution—were all fighting for prime time on the new decade's highlight reel.

The Sex Pistols had died for somebody's sins, but unlike other saviors, they stayed dead. Which left the Rolling Stones with precious little left to prove. Such is the curse of winning, I suppose.

All on the wrong side of thirty, the Stones were senior citizens by contemporary rock standards. Hell, Lester Bangs had declared

---

It was far beyond sloppy, it was *egregious*. They were completely lost at sea—Keith plays the opening riff, and Mick's job was to come in right on the top, a heartbeat before Charlie kicks in, but he misses his cue; maybe he couldn't hear the band, who knows, but it left half the guys changing chords where the song was *supposed to be*, and the other half not knowing what to do. And this goes on for *an extended period of time*, with Keith stabbing at it with Chuck Berry riffs, which sounds kind of cool but does very little to help—it is all just a terrifying mess. Charlie vamps it, he jazzes it, and then he massages it some more, and it only gets increasingly fucked up as it goes along. At some point it's like they've completely lost any sense of the "one." And then somehow Keith vibes it, and like a knife thrower at the circus waiting for the lady strapped on the wheel to come spinning around just one more time, so he can land the dagger between her legs and not bury it in her head, he throws it down, just like at the top, taking just a wee bit of flesh off the bone, as he likes to do. Charlie does that thing he does, running the beat up right behind Keith, Mick nails it, everyone falls in together, and once again they are THE GREATEST ROCK'N'ROLL BAND IN THE WORLD. It was sleazy, sloppy, trashy, and unlike anything I had ever heard by a professional rock'n'roll band. It was spectacular, but not what too many people would call *good*. Certainly, there wasn't a bar in the world that would have hired them for playing like that. Personally, I would have bottled that shit—it was magic.

them over the hill and obsolete when they hit with *It's Only Rock 'n Roll* nearly a decade before, the very idea of being taken seriously as a rock musician into the dotage of one's third decade a self-delusional con job. No one could possibly have predicted that baby boomers playing rock music would ever be taken as anything more than a sad joke, *"Hope I die before I get old"* and all that.

Mick, who loved to troll clubs looking for trends to ride, must have been especially frustrated. The sex and rhythm and decadence of the gay disco scene had given way to the corporate version and the new wave of dance music, painted in faux-Day-Glo punk-rock colors, and dripping with increasingly disgusting synthesizers.

As they were, the Stones could have quickly become the vestigial organs of a genre not yet known as *classic rock*, kicked upstairs like executives who'd outlived their usefulness, and placed in stark relief against the void left by Led Zeppelin—defunct due to their irreplaceable drummer dying from complications related to a life lived beyond any reasonable expectation—and the Who, imperiously carrying on despite their irreplaceable drummer dying from same.

This was the beginning of the bad times, the infighting between Mick and Keith that would level the Stones for the better part of the next decade was just beginning to brew, much of it a hangover from Keith's career as the world's most popular heroin addict.

Living in the future, as we do, riding the wave of twenty-first century correctness, hardcore public drug abuse has lost whatever charm it may have once held. I blame Guns N' Roses and Mötley Crüe—two bands who abused even the most basic punctuation—but that is a story for another time.

If anyone could make smack look sexy, it was Keith Richards, who was to heroin what Rita Hayworth was to Max Factor. The truth of it, however, is the truth of all junkies, because the dope doesn't care what band you play in, it doesn't care how rich you are, it eats you alive. Keith's sublime autobiography pulls no punches—it is as harrowing a tale of heroin addiction, living fix to fix, and dodging (mostly) the long of the arm, as it is the story of a rock'n'roll band. It's right up there with the first tier of junkie memoirs, the sorts of darkly romantic nightmares scribbled by Art Pepper or Anita O'Day.

And if you had some idea that the Stones' heroin days burned hardest during the *Exile* period, or that there is some wonderful romance to being a slave to the drug, well, that may only be because back in that particular dirty filthy basement, Keith was surrounded by too many likeminded or easily corruptible cowboys, and that so many good songs across the most creative decade of their career seemed to blossom directly from the color palette of the lifestyle. Mick was never as hell-bent on drink and drugs as the guitar players (in fact, he was a notoriously lousy drinker). He was much better at painting the picture than partaking, and used coke and speed and smack the way Van Gogh used cerulean, magenta, and cyan, to craft "Sister Morphine," "Rip This Joint," "Dead Flowers," Can't You Hear Me Knockin'," "Brown Sugar," "Let It Bleed," "Respectable," and on and on, and all this *after* the innocent jabs of "Mother's Little Helper" and the thankfully brief LSD years.

But by the other side of the *Some Girls* follow-up, *Emotional Rescue*, Keith was newly clean, and, free of the itching that comes with detox, he was itching to get on the road. Ronnie, on the other hand, was in full-tilt party mode, carrying on a love affair with free-base cocaine, and between it all, Mick wanted little to do with them, the Heckle and Jeckle of personal chemical warfare, two people whose greatest fear could be summed up by any bottle that was labeled FOR EXTERNAL USE ONLY.

A large part of Mick's job was putting up with these magpies. But by the end of the '70s, having done his job with more genuine verve and glamour than anyone who had come before him, he figured it was time for a break. And then, presumably, he saw the numbers—zoinks! This would be their biggest tour ever, setting a record not by scoring the most groupies but by hooking a big-money corporate sponsor and selling the most tickets. This was increasingly the kind of hot stuff that really got his rocks off, and with a reassurance that someone would keep an eye on Ronnie's crack pipe,[2] they were off to the races with a brand new tour, keeping their unwritten covenant of touring the United States every three years.

For this circus to work, they needed a new record. The machinations of the music industry at the time required a new album to launch a tour. It was just the way things were done, the way things had always been done, since the beginning of time, since dinosaurs walked the Earth—it would be years before anyone realized that the Stones didn't actually need a new record to tour, and often were better off without one.

With little time, and even less desire to regroup and start the process of writing a new Stones record, they sent their longtime

2 I've heard that it took Keith putting a gun to his head to get him back on the straight and narrow.

engineer, Chris Kimsey—another unsung hero of this story, who'd worked with them since *Sticky Fingers*, and helped make *Some Girls* a stripped-down masterwork—to do a hard-target search for odds and sods, the detritus of the last four or five records, because, as we've come to learn, when the Stones were on, their turds were better than the next guys' dinner.

But even to the Stones, *Tattoo You* must have seemed like a gift, like finding a wad of bills between the cushions of your couch. "I think it's excellent," Mick later said. "But all the things I usually like, it doesn't have. It doesn't have any unity of purpose or place or time."

Leftovers were found from *Goats Head Soup*, *Black and Blue*, *Some Girls*, and *Emotional Rescue*. An amazing bounty, all it required was a good polish.

The smartest thing they did was to give Charlie's snare drum the sound of the gods, the sound of lighting bolts being hurled from Olympus, and this was done not with snazzy electro-computer technology but by trashing it up, sending the track with his snare drum through a remote speaker in the bathroom, and re-recording it as it bounced around the room. It wasn't quite the echo chamber at Gold Star Studios, but the result was an attack the likes of which haven't been heard since Martha Reeves cut "Nowhere to Run."

Charlie's rim shots didn't sound so much like machine gun fire as much as they did a *sprang* of bullets bouncing off of marble walls during a bank heist—they rang of danger and were impossible to predict. He was never about muzzle velocity anyway—his charm lay in the danger of the ricochet. Behind him the guitars were snapping, twangier and punchier than they had ever been, as was the bass—

Bill Wyman never sounded better. Kimsey and his partner, producer and mix master Bob Clearmountain, were doing wonders, finding the Stones even as the Stones had trouble finding themselves.

Mick worked largely alone at the Pathé-Marconi studio in Paris, and he must have really loved working without his pesky bandmates getting underfoot, because his performance is flawless and almost disarmingly unpretentious, neither angry nor overwrought in any sense. Having vanquished the punks, the jibes and barbs of *Some Girls* had given way to confident celebration. His falsetto was vibrant, his new lyrics and melody lines fresh, and nothing sounded like it had gathered moss in the vaults.

Released in the summer of 1981, *Tattoo You* was the Rolling Stones' unexpected jewel, their last truly great record. As it was an amalgam of refurbished outtakes from past records cobbled together on one long-player to support a tour, it was a bona fide miracle, with Charlie very much at the center of it all.

In retrospect, you had to see the Ascent of Charlie Watts coming, like a storm rolling in. From the opening hi-hat of "Doo Doo Doo Doo Doo (Heartbreaker)" on *Goats Head Soup*, the three-stroke ruff that launches the jaunt of "If You Can't Rock Me"—the very first thing that you hear on *It's Only Rock 'n Roll*—through the increasingly uncompromised virility of the rhythm on *Black and Blue*, and then the astonishing crackle and intricacy of the drums on *Some Girls*, with each successive record, the recognition that it was as much Charlie as it was Mick or Keith that made a thing *Stonesy*, that Charlie gave them the *zork* that no one else had, was no longer debatable, it was dogma.

It was all laid bare on *Tattoo You*: on every track, Charlie ducked and weaved and found space to move where less-talented drummers would have found themselves on the ropes. As it is with all great superheroes, he had qualities both human and superhuman—there was a fragility to the unevenness of the fills and breakdowns, even as he sounded like he was machine-gunning a mob.

Without resorting to gymnastics, *Tattoo You* is something like the *Kama Sutra* of rock drumming—each drum fill inserted itself from some wonderful new angle. And this is yet another reason Why Charlie Watts Matters—because he knows that just climbing on top and having at it is not dignified. It's what dogs do.

○ ○ ○

"Start Me Up," which began life as a failed reggae jam, evolved into the perfect one-size-fits-all rock song. It hit the perfect tempo for rock radio, upbeat but not threatening, and even though it boosted the chords from "Brown Sugar," it boasted none of the danger—that bit about making "*a dead man come*" was just enough light-hearted sleaze to put it over. Most of all, it sounded like the old Rolling Stones, but buffed and shiny, like a new car rolling off the lot.[3]

---

3 Leave it to the alchemists in the Stones to turn floss into gold, spinning a mangled cock-up into cash: the intro to "Start Me Up" is as famous a near-wreck as ever was on a hit record, completely fucked upon takeoff, and yet brilliantly resolved within the space of a few beats. College-level papers have been written explaining how Keith's opening riff and Charlie's miscued entrance fall together in awkward bliss. Frankly, I always thought it was a put on, an inside joke between Keith and Charlie, but then again, they've never been able to recreate it, or even seem to have tried—remarkably, every tour it seems to come out differently, with the intro a tic longer or shorter before

The real beauty of *Tattoo You* is that Charlie drives every song—his cat-and-mouse breakdowns, his bending of time, his intention and execution, hi-hats opening and closing without warning, perplexing, and without precedent. And aside from the roly-poly blues song, he kicks off each one of the rockers *personally*.

After "Start Me Up," he lights up "Hang Fire" (which somehow survived the sessions for both *Some Girls* and *Emotional Rescue* before appearing here) with a jagged blast of accelerating sixteenth notes, throwing a ton of dirt in the air with a flurry of wildly inconsistent accents. It was terrific, but also the kind of thing most drummers would get fired for. Throughout the song, the snare drum crackles in the most unexpected places—it is impossible to anticipate, let alone penetrate.

---

the drums tumble in. The amazing thing is, they've kept it so loose—even when it is timed to pyrotechnics, which must be a real pain in the ass to play to. As Keith told *Guitar Player* magazine, "Rock and roll is in one way a highly structured music played in a very unstructured way, and it's those things like turning the beat around that we'd get hung up on when we were starting out: 'Did you hear what we just did? We totally turned the beat around [*laughs*]!' If it's done with conviction, if nothing is forced, if it flows in, then it gives quite an extra kick to it. … You can do that in a band that's got enough confidence not to collapse when it happens." See "Starfucker," above, but also the long intro to "Little Queenie" on *Ya-Ya's*, which starts off right away, with the beat upside down, and requires a bit of ultra-suave Charlie alacrity to right the ship—you can hear him fix it with an extra beat when the vocals come in. It is especially amazing since the record was compiled from three shows, and yet this is the version they chose to include? Almost makes one think it was intentional …

On "Slave," Charlie strides out first and dominates the groove throughout. Originally recorded for *Black and Blue*, with Billy Preston and Ollie Brown's funk still very present on the track, it was now new and improved with saxophonist Sonny Rollins overdubbing the solo, which must have sent ol' jazzbo Watts into orbit. "Little T&A" is Keith's dirty rockabilly, and Charlie cues off of him with two short shots reminiscent of "Rip This Joint." "Neighbours" (like "Little T&A" a refugee from *Emotional Rescue*) was a full-tilt grinder, with Charlie and Mick both swinging for the fences—the intro is a glorious vocal and drum scrimmage, the punk-rock version of "Loving Cup." Sonny Rollins was back, except that jazz hour was over—the snare drum was amped practically to the point of over-modulation.

Side two of the record ("side two" being another twentieth-century micro-anachronism, a subset of the long-playing phonograph record) was the seducer, a suite of ballads that went back as far as *Goats Head Soup*, and Charlie was no less spectacular—that is unless you like your drums whipping around like a tempest in a prog-rock teapot, which was still very much in fashion. Despite the best efforts of disco and punk, minimalism was never a mass movement—Kansas, Rush, Styx, and Yes were still filling arenas—and their overequipped drummers wallpapering the pages of the popular drumming magazines. Charlie had no part in this, still doing surgery on his round-badge Gretsch kit, which looked minuscule compared to the multi-drum installations that were still all the rage.

And every song, no matter how laid-back, had plenty of spine. Every touch of the drums was sympathetic to the song—Charlie could put Mick over like no one else. There was a musical dynamism on this stuff that bested even the Stones' classic ballads and weepers. *Tattoo You* was the record no one saw coming. Once again, Charlie cut across punk rock and rockabilly, blues, jazz, and country, slashing with precision, removing hearts before a drop of blood could hit the floor.

o o o

Unfortunately, if the Rolling Stones' 1975 Tour of the Americas had expanded the artistic possibilities of working in hockey arenas by crafting a stage show that cunningly managed to keep the sex and sleaze high in the mix—what with the vaginal, blossoming lotus stage (genuinely cool) and the giant inflatable penis (genuinely stupid, but fun)—the 1981 US tour denatured it all with pastel colors, balloon drops, and a cherry picker for Mick. Because just in case you didn't get the point that it was *his* show, he had now hired a hydraulic lift so he could float a hundred feet over the crowd, like Eva Perón in a fever dream.

This is where all the druggy show-business decadence of the last tours went to die. They had nothing left to prove, and it showed. They had a great record behind the tour, but, as Mick said, there was no "unity of purpose or place or time" to it, and you could feel it when they took it on the road.

This was the first tour where Keith didn't really dig into his guitar like he was chopping up bodies. Mostly he seemed content enough being Keith Richards—it was a goddam miracle that he was there at all—but he was *voguing*, not *slashing*. He was mugging, and not in the good sense, i.e. committing a street crime.

Mick's new policy of running to and fro was taken to the extremis, and as much as the audience went nuts for all of that jazzercise, it wasn't doing much for the lad's singing—he seemed to be out of breath, or that could have just been his new sense of urgency for the 1980s. Reagan and Thatcher did have their way of making everyone nuts.

Ronnie spent as much time slurping cocktails and incessantly smoking cigarettes as he did playing the guitar with any sense of real purpose. It bordered on the irresponsible—a tough line to cross if you are the guitar player in the Rolling Stones.

It was a nice treat that Bobby Keys was allowed out of his cell to blow the solo on "Brown Sugar," and great to see original Stone Ian Stewart on piano and ex-Faces Ian McLagan on organ (the whole organization was lousy with ex-Faces), but, truly, it was only Charlie Watts holding it together with any sense of real urgency, undaunted by the lack of joyfully murderous spirit one had come to hope from these affairs.

Once upon a time, the Stones would roar out of the gate, down to fuck. This time, with so many children in the audience, not to mention backstage—the pitfalls of becoming a global, trans-generational entertainment attraction—they settled for something a bit more bouncy, the musical equivalent of one of those inflatable castles parents rent for their kids' backyard birthday parties. This was a sexless version of the Rolling Stones, a family-friendly outing where ice cream cones with sprinkles were as likely to be consumed by the audiences as sloppily rolled joints of Mexican brick weed and cheap hashish in hot metal pipes.

The resulting live record, aptly titled *Still Life*, was not much more than a cheap souvenir (*Rolling Stone* called it "the aural equivalent of a Stones T-shirt, the final item of tour merchandise"), a quickie job that tipped their hand at how much they thought of the whole *megillah*. It was a cash grab first, cultural artifact second, and, what's worse, it felt like it. *Still Life* isn't the only mediocre Rolling Stones record that I initially bought with enthusiasm, and then only listened to later for the drums, but it was the first.[4]

Charlie was truly that tree planted by the waters, the one whose leaves were green, and who feared not when the heat came, and was not anxious in the drought, and never ceased from yielding fruit. And this is just one more reason Why Charlie Watts Matters, because you could always count on him to deliver, even when everyone else has lost their fucking minds.

---

4 The few bright spots of the show were the throwaway cover of "Twenty-Flight Rock," a perfectly enjoyable toss-off of the Eddie Cochran song, with wonderfully snapping drums—a lesson in old-school syncopation and modern primitivism that zipped by far too quickly—and an honest attempt at turning the heat up on "Let Me Go," an excellent second-tier country song from *Emotional Rescue*. On one hand, it kept the country-punk ethos of *Some Girls* alive, but sadly, few in the audience had any idea what they were doing, and, in the end, it didn't seem like the Stones did, either. No one knew better than they did that while some songs cut harder when you stepped on the gas, just as many lost their mojo when you went over the speed limit. The fact that they believed in "Let Me Go" enough to put it in the set spoke well to their good taste; the fact that they felt the need to play it at twice its natural tempo said little for any remaining confidence in their own natural swagger. And the less said about the Smokey Robinson cover, "Going to a Go Go," the better.

Charlie on form, 1981. (Photofest)

TEN

WHERE'S MY DRUMMER?

NOW IT'S TIME TO TELL THE STORY, the one everyone loves to hear, about Charlie Watts coming down from his hotel room in the middle of the night, freshly shaved, dressed to the nines in his best Savile Row suit, and slugging Mick Jagger in the jaw.

It is a very good story, and true. You cannot beat the Charlie Watts right hook. It's like being hit by a freight train. Think about him playing "Rip This Joint" on the side of your skull, and you begin to get the idea.

This is the beginning of the bad times. Keith is clean, and while Mick has been doing a championship job holding things together with a world-class junkie as his second, by the time they come out the other side, he is convinced the Stones are his band, and the last thing in the world he wants is to cede control to a cleaned-up junkie guitar player now capable of sharing the decision making.

It's only a few months after the 1981 tour, but by this point, Mick and Keith aren't even talking to each other, heels dug into the argument that will define the confusion of their work for years: Mick wants to make a trendy pop record heavy on dance music, and Keith wants to stick to their roots and drive the guitars into the earth. Blues, reggae, rock'n'roll, whatever, just no tricks. He doesn't care what the kids are listening to—he cares about what the Rolling Stones do best.

Nonetheless, they set up again at Pathé-Marconi in Paris, and generally Mick would come in from noon to five, Keith would show up around midnight and work till dawn, and when one was around and the other wasn't, which was pretty much always, they took to erasing each other's parts.

Somehow they managed to squeeze out *Undercover* in 1983, the beginning of their increasingly declining creative output, and their first subpar record with Ronnie Wood, although there would be plenty more. Like all of their successive records, you could find a few good moments on it worthy of the Stones imprimatur (and lots of great drumming): the title track wasn't so bad, for instance—lots of cool guitarring—but it was so obviously pandering to MTV that whatever its good intentions may have been, they were been buried beneath a laboratory's worth of synths and sequencers. Keith went along with Mick, but he also spat that "it sounded to me like a rehash of something he heard in a club one night."

The situation only got worse as Mick Jagger began his solo career.

The Rolling Stones had a brand new recording contract, and

somehow Mick Jagger comes out of the negotiations with a huge deal for *himself*, to do a pile of solo records for scads of dough, and World War III ensues.

Keith sees this as something far beyond sedition. It is mendacious, dishonest and disrespectful, a knife in the fucking back. No one is bigger than the band. They built this *cosa nostra* together, and now Keith feels betrayed, and Charlie, whose sense of loyalty to the band is as deep as the ocean, feels worse than Keith. This according to Keith, who is on a homicidal rampage.

Everyone has had it with Mick. The deal got piggybacked on the Stones' new record deal in the middle of the night, when no one was watching, and that's not how shit gets done. As anyone who has ever seen *Goodfellas* knows, "You had to have a sit-down, and you better get an okay, or you'd be the one who got whacked."

But Mick just went rogue in his bid to become the next Michael Jackson or David Bowie, because he had some record-company suit in his ear, telling him how huge he could be.

He especially worshipped David Bowie, who played by his own rules and wasn't stuck working with the same band for fifty years, and who moved easily between worlds as a professional weirdo, international fashion icon (more like *interstellar* fashion icon), rock-star royalty, and could have massive dance hits and still be respected as a legit *artiste*. Where do you think Mick got the idea for all that gender bending in the early 1970s? It was a hardcore crush, the Jagger/Bowie thing. Of course, unlike Bowie, Mick was no *avant-gardist*—he had none of the cultural fearlessness of Bowie, and he was way too obsessed with being on trend to experiment—

not to mention, *his brand was the Rolling Stones.* Somehow, Mick saw this not as the greatest blessing ever bestowed upon a former economics student but "a millstone around his neck," as he snarked to a British tabloid.[1]

Keith went berserk when he heard that comment: "Disco boy, Jagger's Little Jerk Off Band, why doesn't he join Aerosmith?" Keith was never one to pull punches.

Which brings us back to Charlie slugging Mick. Everyone knows the story. It's odd: decades of playing the drums for the Rolling Stones, and *this* is the story everyone loves to tell? Is it because it speaks truth to power? Everyone likes to hear that the urbane drummer is not to be fucked with. Anyway, it is funny—it's got so much Charlie *zork!*—but everyone seems to forget the, uh, *punch line.* So here it is.

It's 1984, the Stones are not getting along at all, but they're trying to patch things up, and they find themselves in Amsterdam for a meeting. Mick and Keith are on lousy terms, but they decide to go out for a few—a few being Mick's limit. Anyway, Keith lends

---

1 Bowie, "solo act" that he was, was extremely loyal to certain band members—no less his drummer, Dennis Davis, a monster who could play Bowie's mess of R&B and experimental rock flawlessly and with great style, and, obviously, get along with his boss, who kept him around for an astonishing string of records and tours, from Bowie's own mid-'70s foray into the Philly Sound, *Young Americans,* through the Berlin years—*Low, "Heroes",* and *Lodger*—all the way to *Scary Monsters.* Bowie was a genius at putting together great bands—he knew the value in creating a viable, working group, and holding them together. Jagger had at least twenty-five musicians on his first solo record, including six drummers (not counting percussionists), and seven different people playing synthesizer parts.

Mick a jacket to go out, the one Keith got married in, and they get back to the hotel around five in the morning, properly potted. At which point Mick has the bright idea, against Keith's sage advice, to call up to Charlie's room and demand, "Where's my drummer?"

According to Keith, "Twenty minutes later, there was a knock at the door. There was Charlie Watts, Savile Row suit, perfectly dressed, tie, shaved, the whole fucking bit. I could smell the cologne! I opened the door and he didn't even look at me, he walked straight past me, got a hold of Mick and said, 'Never call me your drummer again.' Then he hauled him up by the lapels of my jacket and gave him a right hook."

Keith calls it the "drummer's punch" and says "it's lethal; it carries a lot of balance and timing." Nothing less than you would expect from a guy whose right hand has been carrying the weight of The GREATEST ROCK'N'ROLL BAND IN THE WORLD for twenty years.

So far, so good. But here's the part everyone forgets: the Charlie Watts right hook is in fact no laughing matter, and Mick flies back onto a platter of smoked salmon and begins to slide out the open window toward the canal below—and admit it, *Mick Jagger sliding out a window on a platter of smoked fish into a canal is fucking hilarious*. After all the drugs, the misadventure, Altamont, and every other fucked-up situation that they have ever been in, who thought this is how the Rolling Stones would end, in a scene more worthy of a Marx Brothers movie than *Cocksucker Blues*?

Except that Keith realizes that Mick is wearing *his* jacket, *the one he got married in*, and he really wants it back. It's a real "leave the gun, take the cannoli" moment. Keith grabs Mick and hauls him back into the room. Charlie is incensed—he was happy to see Mick go flying out the window. In fact, he wants to have another go at it, but Keith is *insistent* about not wanting to lose the jacket.

o o o

Saving Mick's life, oddly, does not improve things. Keith, that sentimental fool, continues his rampage against Mick, whom he now regularly refers to as "Brenda," or "Madam," or "Her Majesty." He's had it. His basic outrage is that if Mick wanted to make a record of Irish lullabies with Liberace—something he couldn't have done with the Stones—well then, have at it, but "if he doesn't want to go out with the Stones and then goes out with Schmuck and Ball's band instead, I'll slit his fucking throat." It's a low moment for the Stones, but you couldn't say it didn't make for good copy. Someone asked Keith, "When are you two going to stop bitching at each other?" and Keith's response was, "Ask the bitch."

There was a huge amount of publicity surrounding Mick's first solo record, *She's the Boss*, what with MTV and the entire musical-industrial complex behind him (not to mention all of the trash talk that kept him in the papers), but as a wise man once said, "For what shall it profit a man, if he shall gain the whole world, and lose his own soul?" Another wise man, namely Keith, said, "It's like *Mein Kampf.* Everybody had a copy, but nobody listened to it."

Certainly, nobody who did remembers it—which is fine, pop music is largely disposable by design—but this is why God gave him the Rolling Stones. There was no need for Mick to run off to make bad pop/rock records—the Stones were quite capable of doing it themselves. Mick actually makes four of these fucking things, with precipitously diminishing returns (before eventually issuing the completely inessential and erroneously titled *The Very Best of Mick Jagger*,[2] a contractual obligation, one can only assume). But the harm is done—for the next few years, the Rolling Stones are effectively doing their best impression of Schrödinger's cat, and Keith is in murder mode.

The odd thing is that it wasn't unprecedented for the Stones to make solo records. Bill Wyman was first, way back in 1974, with *Monkey Grip*, which was a good-natured-enough rock'n'roll record with lots of heavy friends—Lowell George, Dr. John, Leon Russell, etc. It was a perfectly pleasant affair—Bill can actually write very decent pop/rock'n'roll songs, and obviously enjoyed doing so, something that was not really going to happen within the Jagger/ Richards songwriting empire. It even came out on their own label, Rolling Stones Records, so it had the family blessing. It got a few good reviews, Bill got to shine for a few moments, and no one cared. He followed it up a couple of years later with more of the same on *Stone Alone*, which was about as good as a middling Ringo Starr record, if not actually as charming. It too came out on the Stones' own label, and no one cared. In 1981, Bill had a minor hit with the synth-driven dance-drivel novelty record "(Si Si) Je Suis Un Rock Star." It was funny enough, and harmless, and it made it into the British Top 40, and no one cared.

---

2 Inessential as it already existed. It was called *Exile on Main St.*

Ron Wood had been putting out solo records for years. *I've Got My Own Record to Do* (1974)—from the sessions that produced "It's Only Rock 'n Roll"—sounds pretty much what you would expect the Faces' guitar player's solo record to sound like, but even with his posse of rock star pals sitting in, within a few songs you are kind of left wondering why you aren't actually listening to the Faces. *Gimme Some Neck* came out the year after *Some Girls*, and is a lot of fun—having Charlie on the drums (not to mention Mick and Keith and Bobby Keys sitting in) didn't hurt, although after a few listens you are left wondering why you aren't actually listening to the Rolling Stones. Of course, Ronnie wasn't officially a Rolling Stone then, so no one cared. He's put out a few more things of lesser quality since then, for what reason your guess is as good as mine, but everyone likes Ron—he's like a puppy that loves to play—but he's a perennial sideman, and no threat to anyone.

And then there is Keith. Oh, Keith, what to say?

Keith never saw himself making rock'n'roll records outside of the Rolling Stones—for what?[3] But Mick ran off to join the circus, and suddenly Keith was a man driven to put together a working band, make a record, and get it out on the road.

Everyone said they loved Keith's first record, *Talk Is Cheap*, but mostly everyone loves Keith. He is a man of the people, and at

---

3 Keith had actually put out a solo single in 1978, and no one had a heart attack over that, either. It was just a good-natured Christmas single, "Run Rudolph Run," with a horrendous but highly enjoyable version of "The Harder They Come" on the B-side, with Ronnie on drums, obviously having a great time.

The Charlie Watts Big Band. (Dick Loek/ Toronto Star via Getty Images)

least while Mick was presumably busy scouring marketing reports, wearing half-moon glasses and a monogramed silk robe while a white-gloved butler kept busy ironing his copy of the *Wall Street Journal*, Keith was out on the road, slurping Jack Daniel's and playing rock'n'roll music with a bunch of guys he genuinely likes.

But back to our hero. The remarkable thing—or perhaps the most unsurprising thing—is that Charlie Watts is the only Rolling Stone who could make a run of perfectly lovely solo records that are beyond criticism.

He might as well be doing the record of lullabies with Liberace—that's the genius of Charlie Watts. There is no agenda. *Ars gratia artis*—he's doing it because he loves it. It is pure of spirit in every possible way.

Aside from occasionally playing with Ian Stewart and Jack Bruce in their boogie-and-blues bar band Rocket 88 in the late '70s and early '80s, Charlie began his solo career in the most spectacular way, with the Charlie Watts Orchestra in 1985, and, no kidding, it was a BIG BAND, over thirty people, including three trap drummers—Charlie was front and center, flanked by the other two—plus an army of horns, including the best British boppers, old-school cats, and unrepentant modernists, turning in enthusiastic versions of big-band and bop classics like "Stomping at the Savoy," "Lester Leaps In," "Scrapple from the Apple."

I remember seeing them at the Ritz in New York City, and the most striking thing about them was Charlie's smile. It took over the room—I have genuinely never seen a man seem so happy.

It was a dazzling band—just the sheer size of the thing was awe-inspiring—and in the middle was Charlie, swinging along, but mostly the other two cats on drums were doing the heavy lifting. Charlie, who never took a drum lesson, isn't much for reading charts—he let the sidemen drop the bombs and throw the big hits—but he was just having the time of his life, driving this gigantic jazz machine.

After turning out a live recording of the big band, he eventually settled down with his Quintet, co-starring his school chum Dave Green, who'd be a part of all of these projects, on bass. Dave was around when Charlie took the neck off of that old banjo, and sat listening to Charlie Parker 78s with him when they were kids, and they were still at it.

In 1991, they revamped Charlie's children's book, *Ode to a*

High Flying Bird, as a limited CD, *From One Charlie*. It's lovely and odd, like the artist himself, just twenty-eight minutes of well-heeled bebop including a reprint of his original artwork, and it is a joy in every possible way, as a tribute, as part of a childhood dream finally fulfilled, as a stand-alone jazz disc. Charlie is not an overpowering jazz drummer, but he swings easily, and the group falls together naturally, with his childhood buddy on bass, to whom he is exceptionally loyal, and the highly accomplished and smooth-sounding Peter King—the outstanding British alto player who has worked with everyone from Philly Joe Jones and Anita O'Day to Ray Charles—playing the role of Bird, capturing the mood and somehow avoiding the astringent weirdness that Parker sometimes flaunted.

A Tribute to Charlie Parker with Strings, recorded live on two consecutive nights at Ronnie Scott's new venue in Birmingham the year before, featured Stones backup singer Bernard Fowler reading a little bit of narration from "Ode to a High Flying Bird"—the first half of the CD is the Quintet doing a live version of *From One Charlie*, the second, fresh material with the string section. Most of the songs were written by Charlie's ace-in-the-hole, Peter King, with a handful of Charlie Parker tunes peppering the set, making it far more than a set of covers or a purist's tribute act. *Variety* called it "the most artistically successful solo project by any Rolling Stone."

Charlie was obviously living a dream, sitting behind a top-flight jazz band, with a convincing crooner warbling his favorite tunes, and surrounded by strings. "You sit and the strings just swell,"

Jazzbo Charlie Watts, the accidental rock star.
(Continuum Records)

he told *Rolling Stone*, "it's a fantastic sound to just swish away to. I enjoy that because I play with guitar players all the time." One could almost feel the tension of his day job melting away.

Warm and Tender (1993) was sixteen standards with Bernard

Fowler on vox and even more strings—an entire freaking orchestra, in fact. The Charlie Parker influence had receded to the background, and the follow-up, *Long Ago and Far Away* (1996), ditto, delivered on its promise—it is lush, Romantic in both senses, and sexy in a very old-fashioned way. It's beautiful, but it moves so slowly it would likely make most Rolling Stones fans want to kill themselves.

When the Charlie Watts Quintet became a working reality, between Stones tours in the early 1990s, Charlie also started showing up on television, seemingly out of character for "the quiet Stone." Famously press-shy, he was never game to talk about his steady gig, but he felt like he had to go old-school with his jazz bands and get the word out. He had the same reasonable fear as any other jazz musician in the latter part of the twentieth century— that the only people in the audience on any given night might be his wife and his best mate.

But he was treated with godlike reverence, even as he disarmed talk-show hosts with his good manners, dry wit, and refusal to talk about the Rolling Stones, preferring to proselytize about Dave Tough and Charlie Parker, Chico Hamilton and Big Sid. There was little hope that anyone in the audience had any idea what he was talking about, but when the Quintet started playing, everyone was charmed.

Let's be very honest here: with few exceptions, what chance does a jazz musician have of getting to play on a mainstream television talk show, let alone sit on the couch for the interview?

But not everything in this world is equal. Being a Rolling

Stone has its perks—you just didn't realize until now that it meant bringing your jazz combo on to late night talk shows. And if a few people got turned on to Bird, or went out to a jazz club, then, aside from having a good time, Charlie was doing the Lord's work. The early Stones felt the same way—blues evangelists bringing the Gospel to the masses—and it worked. It got me making secret trips into New York City to scour dusty record bins in the back of Disc-o-mat for Howlin' Wolf and Ike & Tina records before I had even kissed a girl, and to Muddy Waters and B.B. King shows before I was old enough to drive.

The Charlie Watts Quintet played Ronnie Scott's in London and the Blue Note in New York, toured North America, Europe, and Japan, and it only got bigger, in size and popularity. For a few moments, the band swelled to a tentet, and Charlie put out another live disc, *Watts at Scott's*. At this point, between his solo records, turns with Howlin' Wolf and Ronnie Wood and Leon Russell, and bits and pieces sitting in here and there, he has played on more good records than Mick Jagger.

As it turned out, Charlie Watts, *sans* Stones, was adored—the mystique of being the one guy in the group who didn't spend his entire allowance on eyeliner, who was genuinely shy, whose threads spoke to gentility and not decadence, and who played the drums with a humility that would have been unnerving if it weren't so fucking suave (he was also an inveterate, old-school stick twirler), was, in its own urbane way, a very powerful thing.

Once again, he was practically redefining the music in its simplicity. Despite his ability to rock football stadiums, he didn't come to the jazz world with the torrential power of Elvin Jones or Tony Williams, and he didn't control the weather like Kenny Clarke or Roy Haynes, who could create hailstorms bebopping their way to ecstasy at high velocity. But there was a natural swing to his playing, born of a pure love for the music, and forged by years straddling the snare drum. He was never anxious—there wasn't much approaching *penetration* in this music—and he held a near-religious reverence for *anything* jazz, one that he thankfully left behind with the Stones.[4]

With his Quintet, Charlie was often just content to "stir the soup," moving the brushes across a rough-coated snare-drum head, a lot like Chico Hamilton did on "Walkin' Shoes," the first record that inspired him; or simmer on the ride cymbal, occasionally throwing down the backbeat, like Jimmy Cobb did

---

4 *The Charlie Watts / Jim Keltner Project* is the outlier in the Watts solo discography, an oddball record of drums overdubbed on drums, mangled with sequencers, samplers, and other percussion—pots and pans, Indian drums, apparently anything that was laying about—that Charlie made with his good friend, the neo-platonically perfect drummer Jim Keltner. It sounds something vaguely like abstract African electronica, if that is actually a thing. Every track is named after a drummer they love—Shelly Manne, Tony Williams, Kenny Clarke, etc.—although it has seemingly very little to do with any one them. And yet this is one more reason Why Charlie Watts Matters—he seems to be the only one of this crew with no fear of the *avant-garde*, no hang-ups about drawing outside the lines, experimenting, or making art for art's sake. In 1968, he had even financed and produced a record by the British collective of free-jazz hippies, the People Band, who created the kind of far-out noise that terrified even hardcore jazz fans and acid-heads. Personally, I think it's a pretty cool record, and that Charlie encouraged this ensemble of musical lunatics speaks well of him, but hearing it once was plenty.

on Earl Bostic's version of "Flamingo," his other early fave.[5] But in 2009 he put together a jazz-and-boogie band that blew the doors out—the absolutely ecstatic ABC&D of Boogie Woogie, featuring two pianos, bass, and drums. Charlie was back to shuffling like a madman on the brushes, or swinging wildly on the ride cymbal, driving it like he used to do in the early days of the Stones when they were still cranking on "Down the Road a Piece," now returned to glory on the ABC&D disc *Live in Paris*. It rocked hard, without guitars, just like old times when the distance between jazz and rock'n'roll was still measured in short breaths.

In 2017, he issued what was possibly his best effort, *Charlie Watts Meets the Danish Radio Big Band* (recorded in 2010), a Gil Evans–like suite that featured a turn on a few Stones riffs ("Satisfaction," "Paint It Black," "You Can't Always Get What You Want"), making the whole thing sound like the soundtrack to a druggy noir that desperately needed to be made.[6]

Charlie Watts playing the drums is the sound of happiness, the aural equivalent of Snoopy doing his dance of joy. It was never about chops, it was about style. And no drum solos! It was a good reminder to anyone still stuck on blinding technique as the measure of a great musician: *it don't mean a thing if it ain't got that*

---

5 Cobb went on to play with Miles on *Kind of Blue* and *Sketches of Spain*, not to mention years with Sarah Vaughan, etc., etc., but he knew how to slam the *two* and the *four* when that's where the money was.

6 In an inspired bit of casting in an otherwise dismal movie, principal members of the Charlie Watts Quintet are featured in the 1992 film *Blue Ice*, starring Michael Caine as a former spy turned jazz-club owner.

swing. It is not ironic that these are also the lessons taught by punk and country, and rock and blues. By now you know the story—it's all the same shit.

In many ways, the Rolling Stones at their best were a more intense jazz band than Charlie's actual jazz bands[7]—when the Stones were cooking, not a lot got played the same way twice. There was more group improvisation. They weren't *jamming*, not in the hippie sense, but in the sense that the roll was still lubricating the rock. They kept it greasy.

Charlie played more aggressive, out-there jazz in the first four bars of "All Down the Line" and the breakdowns of "Rip This Joint" than with any of his jazz combos. There was more improvising and flashing of chops in "Midnight Rambler," when things were going right and Keith and Charlie were doing that thing, changing tempos and mashing up crazy shuffle stops, than there were on any Quintet session.

And this is yet one more reason Why Charlie Watts Matters: even being in the world's most successful rock'n'roll band could not stop him from living his dream.

---

7 Duke Ellington, as is often the case, said it best: "Rock 'n' roll is the most raucous form of jazz."

All grown up, 1994. (Photofest)

ELEVEN

BRIDGES TO
NOWHERE

IN 1983 OR SO, the hero of this story, the drummer who has been the glue in this insanity factory, becomes a full-blown fuck-up.

After years of being partners with the world's most celebrated junkie, but sticking largely to booze and a bit of reefer, Charlie is spending his days high on speed and smack, and drinking like a man hell bent on catching up to his buddy Keith. He is forty-two years old.

Then again, who among us would have the strength *not* to develop a drug and drink problem, after spending their lives with these drama queens?

Actually, the bigger problem is *not* hanging around with them, idle hands and all that. When the Stones began, they were on the industry pace: *make a record, tour, make a record, tour.* That was always the grind. But now there could be *years* between albums. When they finally got around to recording *Undercover*—approximately when Charlie's drinking began to surge—the band was completely dysfunctional.

This is not *Goats Head Soup* fucked-up—this is something entirely different. You've got Keith and Mick not only sniping at each other but actively trying to sabotage each other. Going to the office sucked. Making Rolling Stones records used to be fun. Now it's like digging graves.

Undercover came and went, even if the title track and "She Was Hot" had some staying power in their live sets (the former actually sounded like the Stones having a romp, once all of the electronic splatter was removed, and the latter, when played with a bit of adult dignity, revealed itself to be not so much a goofy pop hit as much as it was another great secret country song). Meanwhile, Mick took off on his solo trip, World War III began (see previous chapter), and suddenly there was an unholy stretch of time with no Rolling Stones.

When Charlie was at home, he lived the life of landed country gentry, largely on his horse farm in Devon, but he has always said he made his wife nuts. "She's wonderful," he told the *Mirror*, "she's something else. She is an incredible woman. She is very good to me, she never made many waves. The one regret I have of this life is that I was never home enough. But she always says when I come off tour I am a nightmare anyway and tells me to go back."

He's an odd guy, Charlie. He is a collector, very big on American Civil War relics, and his collection of old and cool drums, artifacts of the jazz he loves, is legend. He also collects antique cars, but he can't drive. Never got a license. Once in a while he sits in them and runs the engines, but that's as far as he gets.

When tours get shelved and the singer starts threatening to blow up your life's work, you might start taking drugs, too, is all I'm saying.

"Looking back, I think it was a mid-life crisis," Charlie was quoted in *Drum Magazine*. "I became totally another person around 1983 and came out of it about 1986. I nearly lost my wife and everything over my behavior."

For the quiet Stone, he was very open about a very bad time.

This wasn't the first time Charlie had taken a taste—he'd been dabbling with smack during the recording of *Some Girls*, just as Keith was in his final rounds with the drug and facing hard time. "I fell asleep on the floor," Charlie confessed to the BBC. "Keith woke me up and said, 'You should do this when you're older.'"

Charlie quit on the spot, but unfortunately he took Keith's advice to heart and picked it up again six or so years later. When they finally got around to making their next record, *Dirty Work*, he was so fucked-up he could barely play, and they had to call in a couple of ringers to sit in on the drums, including Keith's future bandmate Steve Jordan and session dude Anton Fig. Ronnie Wood even played drums on one track. It took over twenty musicians to finish the record.

Charlie told *Rolling Stone*, "I nearly killed myself. At the end of two years on speed and heroin, I was very ill. My daughter used to tell me I looked like Dracula ...

"I just stopped cold—for me and for my wife. It was never me, really. I passed out in the studio once, and that to me was a blatant lack of professionalism ... I passed out, and Keith picked me up—this is Keith, who I've seen in all sorts of states doing all sorts of things—and he said to me, 'This is the sort of thing you do when you're sixty.'"[1]

Rock bottom came when he broke his ankle going down some stairs to fetch a bottle of wine. "I slipped down the steps when I was in the cellar getting a bottle of wine," he told the *Guardian*. "I happened to be booked for a jazz show at Ronnie Scott's in six weeks' time, and it really brought it home to me how far down I'd gone. I just stopped everything—drinking, smoking, taking drugs, everything, all at once. I just thought, enough is enough."

o o o

Meanwhile, Mick and Keith are still not talking to each other, and with Charlie in the weeds, the state of the band has become a sort of existential conundrum—how do you make a Rolling Stones album *without the Rolling Stones*?

Not surprisingly, *Dirty Work*, foisted on the public in 1986, is a lousy record.

Ironically, it also has the last great Rolling Stones song on it.

I am going to go out on a limb and say, for the record, that the last truly great original Rolling Stones track is "Had It with You," and I can't think of a single Rolling Stones–penned song on any record since then that I ever really need to hear again. When they

---

1 Fortunately, this time Charlie didn't take Keith's advice to kick the drug problem down the road. In 2001, when he turned sixty, Charlie was in great shape, getting ready for the massive Licks tour: 117 shows on five continents in just over a year.

come on the radio I don't switch stations, but does anyone ever come home from work and pop on *Bridges to Babylon*?

"Had It with You" is by far the scrappiest thing they've ever put on a record. Largely just Keith's guitar, with Mick on vox and vindictive harmonica, and Charlie slugging it out (they didn't even bother with the bass track), a hate-filled romp broken in half with the kind of sleazy breakdown they hadn't teased with since "Midnight Rambler."

This is Keith at the peak of frustration, writing a song just for Mick:

I love you, dirty fucker...

And Mick got it, and spat it *hard*. It's amazing how this even snuck under the radar and got by the suits, it is so sonically *raw-boned*. The rest of the record—"One Hit (to the Body)," "Fight," etc.—sounds like the soundtrack to one of the later *Rocky* films, which makes sense, since *Dirty Work* is basically the sound of Mick and Keith fighting.

A lot of the brutality in "Had It with You" is in its honesty—not to mention the drums, Charlie had it together that day—but in the Stones' world, it barely qualifies as a professional recording. It certainly doesn't have the big, plastic, corporate kiss that killed the rest of the record. It's more like a hot take from the avant-blues-garage-punk scene—the underground that spat up bands like the Oblivians, the Gories, and the Jon Spencer Blues Explosion. It's a shame that the whole record didn't sound like that.

o o o

And this is where Keith gets his band together—Mick refuses to tour with the Stones, and carries on with his next record, *Primitive Cool*, which is unsurprisingly neither—and Charlie straightens up and digs into his big-band project. An old-fashioned headshrinker and a stay at Ronnie's favorite celebrity rehab would have been cheaper, but when you are Charlie Watts, you get to choose your therapy, and so he got himself a big band featuring the pick of his favorite jazzers. He started the project climbing out of his dark times, but by the time he brought the show to New York, he was positively radiating happiness.

"My bad period had its downside and its good side," he later said, in the Stones' own oral history. "Without the drugs I never would have had the courage to ask these guys to play with me. ... The jazz orchestra was a good band in the end—during the period we were playing I had cleaned up, so the first phase was completely barmy and the second phase was totally straight: it was the first band I had played in in forty years where I was completely straight."

Eventually, three years after *Dirty Work*, Mick and Keith wake up on the road to Damascus and realize which side of the bread the butter is on, and that the Rolling Stones had better get their narrow white asses back in the studio and start thinking about a record and a tour.

The next record, *Steel Wheels* (1989), is a "comeback"—though it feels like so was everything since Ronnie joined up—and from here on in, it's a blur of increasingly byzantine tours and unfocused studio records, of which every one (the records, that is), with one notable exception, deserves a failing grade.

Of course, sixty percent is a failing grade, so on a twelve-song album, there should be at least 7.2 good songs, which is being kind to the point of absurdity, like telling your ninety-year-old grandmother how much you like her awful, moth-eaten dress.

Steel Wheels isn't terrible, nor is it memorable, but it was incredibly successful, going double platinum in the States. There was definitely a populist movement that wanted the Stones to quit sniping at each other and make a rock'n'roll record.

There are some terrifically exciting moments, but definitely not 7.2 good songs. Likely it is worthy of a "gentleman's C," as they say. More importantly to our story, Charlie is now the *signifier*. The Stones are the *signified*. Mick and Keith are obviously humbled, and they know that whenever they can't get it together, Charlie is the one that is going to make sure that whatever it is, it sounds like the Stones.

Steel Wheels announced itself with a Charlie Watts explosion on "Sad Sad Sad"—an electrifying snare-drum ruff that takes off *behind the beat before the song even starts*, chasing an open-G guitar intro, likely played by Mick, but it's Keith's sound, it's the sound of the Rolling Stones. For my money, it's the best song on the album. Charlie's snare drum sounds bigger than it did on *Tattoo You*—it's not as cool and trashy, but it's definitely become a *thing*.

The drum-and-guitar intro on "Mixed Emotions," the putative hit single, is another fine Stones mindbender. The drums are a frantic Charlie rip on a Motown lick, but the guitar comes in

on the off-beats, giving it the full-tilt wobble before the rest of the band even falls in—itself something of a minor miracle, as it all happens so fast. It is difficult to imagine how anyone could jam that much excitement into about one half-second of music. I could listen to a loop of it all day long, and never mind the song.

It isn't that it is a *bad* song, it's just that they've set the bar so high that what would be a great single for most groups is low tide for the Rolling Stones. They are no longer making what Phil Spector once called "a contribution." Every record has its moments, but you need some sort of divining wand to find them.

But wherever you look, there's Charlie:

On *Voodoo Lounge*, which dropped five years later, in 1994, it's Charlie again, the very first thing you hear on the record. Charlie's intro on "Love Is Strong" is so cool and confident, you start to get the idea that this record might have a fighting chance—a broken roll capped with a small China-cymbal crash, everything you want in the first moment of a Stones song.

The second song, "You Got Me Rocking"—which is what "Going to a Go-Go" should have sounded like—is more of same: Charlie is in before the band, only harder, cranking a bit of snare drum, and then that lovely trashcan cymbal explosion.

Third song, "Sparks Will Fly," more Charlie—and now the third song in a row that starts with him having at it.

And on and on …

He's not suffering in the mix, either—his snare drum is *dominating*. Every time he hits the China cymbal, it sounds like a tree just got hit by lightning. And then, on the last song, "Mean Disposition," he swings it old-school. Pure, big-beat jazz.

What's the message here? Charlie's good tonight, ain't he?

∘ ∘ ∘

Keith had often suggested that anyone who quits the Stones "leaves in a pine box," but by the time they got around to recording *Voodoo Lounge*, Bill Wyman was already gone. Having decided that he could not continue to pretend to be in a teenage rock band, he upped and quit.

Bill was an architect of the Stones' sound, crucial to the wobble, a key player on their best records, but times have changed. Since the Urban Jungle tour supporting *Steel Wheels*, there have actually been more non-Stones onstage than actual Stones—three or four background singers, a three- or four-piece horn section, one or two keyboard players. The sound was very sweetened—if it were a bag of coke, you might say it had been "stepped on"—and a new guy playing bass wasn't going to make that much of a difference. Keith doesn't kill Bill, and, basically, no one cares. Mick. Keith. Charlie. Ronnie. These were the Rolling Stones, and they were still very capable, on any given night, of being THE GREATEST ROCK'N'ROLL BAND IN THE WORLD.

The new guy is Darryl Jones, whom they let Charlie pick. It's a respect thing. Apparently, Charlie digs the fact that Darryl used to play in Miles Davis's band, even though it was in the 1980s, and I would bet they are not the Miles records that Charlie spins on his days off. He also used to play with Sting, but apparently everyone is willing to overlook that.

Darryl leans a little heavier on a traditionally bigger bass sound than the last guy, but it helps fill everything out when Ronnie and Keith are busy preening. Anyway, he's a great bass player, by all accounts a nice guy, and at least they don't make him dress like Bill Wyman.

o o o

By 1997, having logged another tour of galactic proportions, they are back in the studio, but once again they are acting more like petulant children than adults in a professional rock'n'roll band. Mick and Keith are avoiding each other, showing up at different times and running separate sessions. Mick is hustling in hip-hop guys when Keith isn't around, and by the end they aren't even speaking, again. It's fucking tragic, because, you know, when they're getting on they make great records.

But here comes Charlie: once again, the first sound you hear on "Flip the Switch," the first song on their new product, *Bridges to Babylon* (1997), is Charlie, and this time it is an *epic* drum intro—the *shwoop*, a bait and switch between hi-hat and snare, what sounds like the larger China cymbal with rivets (what's known in the trade as a "swish knocker"), followed by a little *zoo-zazz*, a driving beat, another twisted turnaround, and then back to the beat before the guitar drops in—it's like a *suite* of Charlie Wattsisms, practically enough for a ballet, and really quite expansive for an otherwise pro-forma Stones song.

The snare drum is like a radioactive monster on this record. The trashy sound is back, and it is devastating. Unfortunately, there's no jazz to any of this. There are moments—there always are—but it's a disjointed mess. It's hard to tell what anybody was really thinking.

Except, of course, that Charlie's got the mojo hand, and in some sort of attempt to give this thing the *zork* that is so desperately missing, the drums are mixed so loud that it might as well be mistaken for CHARLIE WATTS AND HIS ROLLING STONES.

o o o

I think a lot about Elvis in his final days.

For the last fifteen years of his career, he was seen by hip America as some sort of artifact from the 1950s, a nostalgia act. He belonged to someone's parents, and this was a time when no self-respecting stoner would be caught dead listening to records by an old man, never mind that Elvis was likely the greatest male singer in America, and when he brought the blues, he brought the real deal, learned at the very source. He brought the rock'n'roll *that he invented*. When he sang gospel, he could make you cry.

In 1968, while the Stones were making their statement on *Beggars Banquet*, Elvis went on television, and, channeling Martin Luther King, sang "If I Can Dream," one of the most stirring songs of the civil-rights era, perhaps his most impassioned performance. He was thirty-three years old then, around the same age as the Stones were when they were cutting *Some Girls* and swatting away the punks. But Elvis was considered over the hill and part of the Establishment. His rebel credentials had expired.

On its own terms, "If I Can Dream" was every bit as powerful as "Street Fighting Man" or "Gimme Shelter." Elvis had already led a revolution, now he was calling for *unity*. On the same TV show, it might be noted, he also sang a Jimmy Reed song. Elvis and the Stones were never that far apart. If anything, Elvis was way ahead, glamming it up and getting deep into the eyeliner long before Mick and Keith came around to it. But they both knew that when it came to music, it was all the same shit.

Every rock'n'roll band in the country owed Elvis a great debt—how much did Jim Morrison swipe from him? And how much better was Elvis's band in 1970 than the Doors? *Magnitudes*, I believe is the word you are looking for.

Through the early 1970s, Elvis had one of the best bands on the planet, a crack group featuring Jimmy Page's hero, James Burton, on guitar—early in his career, Page was so enamored of Burton that he kept a photo of him in his wallet—not to mention the incredible Ronnie Tutt on drums, whose thunderous, carpet-bombing intro that kicked off Elvis's stage show every night was like the Las Vegas version of Keith Moon.[2] It's a tragedy that

---

2 Tutt would later do time with the Jerry Garcia Band, which is nothing to sniff at. If there was ever a cat who liked to play slow, it was Garcia. Those tempos were *brutal*. It should also be mentioned that when the Doors woke up and decided they needed some help in the lower register, they hired Elvis's bass player, Jerry Scheff, to play on *L.A. Woman*. He later went on to work with Bob Dylan and Elvis Costello. These guys could not be beat.

American youth in 1972 spent more money on the Doobie Brothers than on Elvis, but such was the state of rock'n'roll culture. No one had heroes then.

Elvis died when he was forty-two. He was a drug addict, but they were different drugs than what were fashionable at the time. I suppose it could be said he was ahead of his time in that department as well.

Had he not died, I assume he'd have carried on, doing pretty much the same thing. More gospel music, for sure. Among his last great sessions was one at the epicenter of soul, the Stax studio, but he was already well on his way out, and he didn't have Keith Richards to kick him in the ass.

The physical and spiritual laws that govern bands are a lot different than those that rule the universe of free agents, like Elvis— or Bob Dylan or Neil Young or Robert Plant, for that matter, just to cherry-pick a few classic-rock icons who put on great shows in their seventies and did not go gently into that good night, never mind Iggy Pop, who hit seventy doing 110. There is some kind of molecular chemistry at work when it comes to *bands*, strong bonds and weak bonds, and this is why Charlie and Keith and Mick matter. It is like building a water molecule: hydrogen and oxygen are plenty sexy on their own, but put them together and you can go swimming.

o o o

Reminder that the Stones were human: in 2004, at age sixty-three, Charlie is diagnosed with throat cancer. He thinks he is going to die. There was a good chance he might. But they caught the cancer early. It took two surgeries and weeks of radiation treatment, and he is a mess, just like any other human, except he is Charlie Fucking Watts, and he comes back *strong*.

"There's suddenly Mick and I looking at each other and going, 'Possibly we're the only two left of the originals,'" Richards told *Billboard*. "[But] you don't talk about that shit, you know? Count on Charlie to be all right, and, fantastically enough, Charlie is incredibly on form … I mean, he's made of cast iron. Charlie came back and he played every rehearsal like it was a show. Amazing, yeah."

If you believe the hype, they sit down facing one another and start writing a back-to-basics rock'n'roll record, *A Bigger Bang* (2005), tracked live on the floor, largely Mick, Keith, and Charlie doing their thing, with all of their old problems now behind them. As if.

The first thirty seconds of the first song, "Rough Justice," are incredible—dirty guitars and a terrific drum blast. It sounds like Charlie is taking off on a rocket to the moon. I could listen to those first moments over and over again.

But pretty soon you get the idea again that this is the Stones sounding like what the Stones think the Stones should sound like. It must be a strange place to live, where you have become such a part of the zeitgeist that you can't escape yourself. It's like running out of clean laundry and having to steal one of your own T-shirts from the merch table. I hear it happened to Picasso all the time.

A Bigger Bang has some nice moments—lots of cool drumming,

as ever—but there is no depth, no real wobble, no weaving, no sense of inspiration other than they needed new product to promote a tour, which included playing the half-time show at the 2006 Super Bowl.

Shine a Light—*still looking good, twirling old-fashioned dirt and sleaze.* (Photofest)

And the hip world thought Elvis was part of the Establishment.

They also made a concert film that year, *Shine a Light*, with Martin Scorsese. Never mind their frustrating recorded output—well into their sixties, the Stones were in remarkably good shape.

The guitars were no longer weapons of mass destruction, and they sometimes got goofy with the posing and studied nonchalance, but they remained the Rolling Stones, the high prophets of blues and soul, not to mention glam, country, and old-fashioned dirt and sleaze, blasting away on "All Down the Line," and turning in a greasy, louche version of "Some Girls," even though the show was a benefit for the Clinton Foundation, the charity of the former American president who was famous for his own girl problems.

It seemed a bit of an elbow in the ribs, what with Bill Clinton being there with his wife and all, but the song didn't seem as nasty as it did in 1978—more like a bawdy song your grandfather might sing after he's had a few too many at Christmas—and the millennial women who have been placed in the front rows as stage dressing (replacing the less photogenic baby boomers that typically fill these seats) were either genuinely turned on, or, more likely, oblivious to what the song was actually about and just thrilled to be there, no matter that the Stones were probably their parents' favorite band.

Mick camps it up with Charlie behind him, mashing his China cymbal between his rubbery, promiscuous fills, selling it like no one else in the world possibly could.

o o o

The years fly by, and the Stones do not stop. There are a handful of tours to follow, all enormous in scope and hype, including the fiftieth anniversary run in 2013, the year Mick and Keith both turn seventy—Charlie is a couple of years older, Ronnie a few years younger—to which Mick Taylor is invited out of the woodpile to play with the band on a run-through of "Can't You Hear Me Knocking," evidence that trying to peel off drug-era jams in a sober age is a high-risk venture.

There are more tours, each one grossing more than the last, and most followed by some sort of souvenir live record, all of which are terribly redundant, but if you are feeling ghoulish and want to compare the 1972 version of "Jumpin' Jack Flash" to the 1999 or the 2012 or 2015 versions, it's all there for you—at last count, the Stones have issued over twenty-five live recordings. Perhaps the most amazing thing is that Charlie never plays it the same way twice.

At least by this time they have figured out that they don't need to keep putting out new studio records to keep the show on the road. The demand for tickets seems to be directly proportional to some imaginary Rock'n'roll Doomsday Clock. The hot blue spark that connected Charlie Watts and the Rolling Stones to antiquity still burned bright, electric blue, but when it was gone, there would be nothing to replace it.

A milestone is a free concert in Cuba in 2016, attended by half a million people.

Cuba is a jewel in their somewhat thorny crowns. It's been a long time since they separated music from politics, but this is a good return—this is all about freedom. Back in the States, the most rebellious thing about the Stones was having the *chutzpah* to charge $500 for a ticket.

Watching the film of their trip, *Havana Moon*, it is hard not to be moved—the response from the Cuban people is one of uninhibited joy. Here they are, the Rolling Stones, ambassadors of a culture that not too long ago would have landed the average Cuban in prison. It is extremely optimistic, the way rock'n'roll was once upon a time, before it became co-opted and corporate and the entire experience was normalized.

Mick continues to run ten miles a night across something so large it can hardly be called a stage. It's more like an aircraft carrier tricked out with giant screens. If a war breaks out, I suppose they will be prepared. To anyone who's been watching the whole time, the band is slowing down, but at the end of the night, it is still the Rolling Stones playing "Jumpin' Jack Flash," Charlie is still chasing Keith, and the massive audience is in rapture. Generations of Cubans are celebrating together. People are crying, and not because of the ticket price.

Rock'n'roll has won, and if you can judge a person by how many people they have touched, and how much joy they have brought into the lives of others, then the Stones' names will all be written in the Book of Life, all past transgressions forgiven.

o o o

As the Stones carried on, the show remained spectacular, often as joyfully sloppy as ever, if not a bit sluggish. But Cuban rock'n'roll revolutions aside, it's what I would call "value neutral." What is "Gimme Shelter" supposed to mean in the twenty-first century? Rape and murder just ain't what they used to be. Neither are slavery or heroin, but is anyone even listening to the words?

A Stones concert had become something of an homage to the past, which made me a little sad, but I'm also reminded that nostalgia is one of those rare things that can swing between the pathological and pathetic (why can't things be like they used to be, back in the good old days?), or be a bonding force, the celebration of a shared experience that brings us all together. What the septuagenarian Stones had in common with the Stones of old is that folks got *very* excited about seeing them, seriously hotted-up with anticipation. Their presence was never taken for granted—these were warriors making very little concession to their age, and they caused a ruckus wherever they went.

If you got to see them in 1969 or the early 1970s, you were witness to a revolution. Things will never be like that again. This is *not* nostalgia, this is not romance, this is *science*—the environment that allowed this sort of rock'n'roll to exist cannot possibly be recreated. Even the audience has changed far too much—the culture couldn't support something so radical. Too much has happened, too much wonder has been taken away. There is no longer any sense of danger in the music.

But even if you caught them across the '80s or '90s, the aughts, or on any of their last tours, as the stages seemed to keep growing in size—that's six decades worth of Stones, so you can't say that you didn't at least have a chance—then you were still an intimate part of this amazing epic, the likes of which will never be seen again. And, if not, you can always cue up *Exile*. Everyone needs a shot of salvation once in a while.

"What the fuck's a rock drummer?" Charlie in 2015, age seventy-four. (Marc Nader/ZUMA WIRE/Alamy)

TWELVE

BLUES IN THE NIGHT

IN 2016, THE STONES WENT INTO THE STUDIO to make a new record, and after taking a trip through the looking glass, they came out with an old one. It was called *Blue & Lonesome* and was a collection of ancient blues songs, and much more of a "return to roots" than *Beggars Banquet* was alleged to have been—innovation, trends, fashion, and politics were nowhere to be found. It was light on decadence. No druggy overtones, no clever production.

The closest they came to rape and murder was a version of Howlin' Wolf's hypnotic one-chord masterpiece, "Commit a Crime," but it still sounded downright evil. It was razor sharp, not an unnecessary note anywhere. The entire record was a minimalist masterpiece. Even Eric Clapton showing up on a couple of songs couldn't ruin it. If you saw a band playing this good in a bar, you'd *plotz*.

The most startling thing, sonically, was Charlie's China cymbal, which exploded across the entire landscape. Sometimes he was just *cranking* on it, leaning into it on the backbeat, splatter painting in an odd shade of blue. It was simultaneously primitive and wildly progressive. It was gorgeously, violently expressionist—a color that didn't usually appear in this part of the jungle—and went that much further in marking Charlie's territory and making these blues their own. It was both futuristic and a throwback to the jazz drummers that Charlie loved, who leaned on that trashy sound to accent the band. It lived in a dimension of imagination, and, as such, *Blue & Lonesome* was perfectly timeless, and a welcome escape from the supercilious bullshit that tanked their previous half a dozen records or so.

We got Mick the no-bullshit, utterly stunning bluesman, and a pride of blues masters who held secret knowledge that easily could have been lost to time.

And, they seemed to genuinely enjoy playing together. It sounded like they were having fun. No one pushed too hard. They were geniuses at this—it is what they had spent their entire lives working toward, the Ancient Art of Weaving. Sure, it was a record of covers—Little Walter, Magic Sam, Jimmy Reed—but they inhabited every song so effortlessly and profoundly, it was as if they were creating them on the spot. It was masterful, like da Vinci sketching a nude, or Michael Jordan making that jump shot.

They delivered one-chord modal grooves that seemed to float, and bent the twelve-bar form to their will, hanging on a chord until they *felt* the change. At other times the bass player moved but the guitar players stayed put. They had a supernatural sense of when *not* to change chords. This is where the country met the city, this is where the earth met the sky.

And the drums! The impossible shuffle was back. How could anyone be so disciplined and so relaxed at the same time? In interviews, Charlie raved about Fred Below to anyone who would listen—"I owe my living to Freddie Below"—and spoke to the jazz of it all, and the difficulty of playing a shuffle correctly.

When I was a teenager and had the bright idea to start playing the drums, I looked to Charlie Watts as a hero—the Rolling Stones were by far my favorite band—and I studied him as arduously as he did Earl Phillips

Big beat in the back seat: the unsurpassed Fred Below, on the road with Little Walter. In the front seat, Walter's driver and an unknown woman. (Photo courtesy Rob Filewicz)

and Fred Below and Chico Hamilton. I also played along with Sabbath and the Who and Zep and Hendrix and Little Richard; also James Brown, Professor Longhair, the MC5, Chuck Berry, and the Ramones, but what Charlie was doing was *beyond*.

Playing along with Zeppelin required learning *parts*—it was very specific and technically advanced. Playing along with the Stones was more like just learning to *play without thinking*. There were stylistic tics but no weird tricks—you just had to let it fly. You had to *dance* with it. The secret jazz of Charlie Watts.

When I got my copy of *Blue & Lonesome*, I decided to have a little fun. I pulled out my own set of gnarled wire brushes, and, short of having a banjo with the neck twisted off, I gave it a go, playing along on an old LP sleeve.[1] It was a hard reality check. I felt handicapped. Physically challenged. The tempos were maddening—the urge was always to push it, but the Stones' magic was *holding it back*. *Anticipation and penetration*. Charlie Watts didn't rise to the occasion, he rose with it.

o o o

When I was coming up, Charlie didn't get much sympathy among other drummers. Nether did Ringo—mostly they got a little respect just for being in the Stones and the Beatles, but very few drummers were singing the praises of these guys. Aside from Bonham, everyone was gaga for Neil Peart and prog-rock octopi with *gazoonga* drum sets who could work ten-minute drum solos.

Times have changed. Charlie is revered. Small drum sets are hip.

Some of it has to do with stripped down, post-punk aesthetics. It's certainly a sign of a return to roots music by young musicians who place a high value on "authenticity" in the face of the industrial pop-music complex, and the realization that this shit cannot be taught, it can only be learned.

---

1 Pro tip: when playing brushes on an LP sleeve, always go for one that has a rough finish, like a coated snare head, for that extra *whooshy* sound. I highly recommend the soundtrack to *The Last Waltz*, which has that nicely pebbled cover and has the added benefit of being a three-record set, making it less likely to fall off of your lap while you are shuffling along on it.

It's an amazing thing: you can look for "How to Play Like Charlie Watts" on the internet and the results are anemic, because none of the drummy dummies who make those sorts of vids can cop his style. There are hundreds of bit-by-bit breakdowns of the most complex Bonham beats, tutorials on insane double-bass-drum parts, intricate jazz lessons, and granular discussions of James Brown's trickiest funk. There is a sub-cult of bedroom drummers playing Neil Peart and Rush songs flawlessly.

But the best you'll get in the Charlie department is a few well-meaning but mostly mistaken cats saying how simple his style is, and showing off the bit about lifting the stick off the hi-hat when he hits the snare drum, or trying to explain the colossal one-two switcheroo at the beginning of "Start Me Up." His style may seem simple to the unenlightened, or to those who still believe the weary claptrap that Charlie and Ringo were just timekeepers, but upon close observation, it baffled all those dudes who had chops like Godzilla but tripped over themselves trying to swing a simple shuffle beat—which is exactly the kind of guys who tended to make videos of themselves playing the drums. Anyway, there is not a lot of wisdom one can gain from watching an instructional video on the internet. If you want to play this shit right, you have to live with it. You have to *commit*.

This is the great flaw of the internet age: *mistaking access to information for knowledge*. Cellphone videos are not a stand-in for experience. Everyone is looking for a shortcut. Charlie Watts came to tell you that they don't exist.

o o o

Through war and peace and disco, they were there. They survived MTV and punk rock, and, if not always one hundred percent relevant, through five decades—in a career that at last count has spanned at least eleven US presidents and twelve or so British prime ministers—the Rolling Stones were always present, and despite whatever problems they had, the infighting and spatting and unwanted hiatus, they never had to call Dio or Donut to fill in. There was *continuity*.

Since their first gig, they have been more consistently successful than the United States military. They were seemingly indestructible. They made it from sweaty basement pubs, playing with Alexis Korner, through the insane early tours, playing over screaming girls at the height of mid-sixties madness, when youth culture meant teenyboppers leaping onstage trying to tear the band to pieces. They survived drug busts, bad psychedelia, and mad and fantastic women. They were witnesses to murder, and complicit in crime. But Charlie was never the one tilting at windmills—he was the one keeping the beat.

That's no trifling gig. The physical demands of drumming are incredible. Hitting a small drum set surrounded by giant guitar amplifiers for a two-hour Rolling Stones set, even with a climate-controlled stage, relaxed tempos, and a good night's sleep behind you, is Olympian shit. There's no posing on this job. No slouching, mugging, or holding power chords while the band plays behind you. You are the band. You stop, the show stops.

Charlie survived cancer and a heroin problem—never mind

that, he's survived being on the road with Keith Richards and Mick Jagger for over fifty years. He never quit when there was plenty of reason to. He had the patience of a fucking saint.

He turned seventy-eight just before the last round of their No Filter tour in the summer of 2019—this just weeks after Mick had heart surgery. Heart surgery![2] They were being written off as old when they were in their thirties, and since then they have been buried and resurrected more than once.

Charlie could have called it quits any time. Bill Wyman made a good call and got out when the getting was good, but he's a different sort of cat. He could always say no to Mick and Keith, but Charlie, not so much—and, anyway, I'm not sure his wife would let him, because then what the fuck was he going to do, mope around the house all day? Well, he always has his jazz combo and his boogie-woogie group. So it was at the beginning, so it was at the end: the Rolling Stones needed Charlie more than Charlie needed them. You couldn't get away with putting some random guy with cat makeup behind the drums and pretend that everything was cool. Thankfully, it wasn't in his character to let people down. Charlie was a gentleman, and he was a soldier.

o o o

We should all gather at my house and talk about how we should feel when we lose the last of our great rock stars. Bring some Jack Daniel's—we're going to need it.

---

2 I blame it on the invention of the wireless mic.

Do you remember where you were when Elvis died? Do you remember where you were when John Lennon was murdered? When you got the news about Prince? David Bowie? Kurt Cobain? Lux Interior? The Ramones? Chuck Berry? And on and on. This is the price of time.

I've met young people who don't know who Frank Sinatra was, never mind that old tosspot Dean Martin. Which will be the first generation that doesn't know the Stones? *There's a hole where there once was a heart...*

The Rolling Stones will not fade away, because the kind of rhythm and sexuality they trafficked in was never based on any trend—it was built from dirt and drugs and decadence and soul, it was Romantic in the grandest sense, and based in ancient knowledge, gained firsthand, from James Brown and Marvin Gaye and Muddy Waters and Howlin' Wolf and Bo Diddley and Little Richard and on and on. The Rolling Stones were the last great band to carry the same torch that was ignited when rock'n'roll was still considered a threat. Ultimately, it will come in and out of fashion, but it will never go out of style.

There was a religious conviction to their best music. They were part of a crusade, and it wasn't without casualties or menace or mistakes, no good one ever is. Sometimes it took a great leap of faith. But if you accept the premise that once upon a time, at least for a moment, the Rolling Stones were THE GREATEST ROCK'N'ROLL BAND IN THE WORLD, then logically—using transitive theory, mereological imperatives, and the practical experience of what we've learned about bands who don't have the right drummer—at least for that moment, Charlie Watts was THE GREATEST ROCK'N'ROLL DRUMMER IN THE WORLD.

But it doesn't matter. Being THE GREATEST, what does it even mean? And who really cares?

What's important is that even when the Rolling Stones were playing Roman Coliseums and Mick was humping a giant inflatable penis or singing from atop a hydraulic cherry picker, when Keith was wasted and Ronnie was close behind, Charlie kicked everyone's ass on his tiny jazz drum kit. He sold the song and looked good while doing it. And this is Why Charlie Watts Matters: you could always count on him to class up the joint. You could always count on him to swing.

We got a good thing goin' … Brian, Mick, Keith, Bill, and Charlie, 1965. (Alamy)

ACKNOWLEDGMENTS

The Rolling Stones, and especially Charlie Watts, are not always keen on giving interviews, and certainly not to lunatics writing unauthorized books, even if they are as spirited and well-intentioned as this one tries to be. Nonetheless, my undying thanks to them for inspiring me in so many ways, especially Charlie Watts, of course, but also to Keith Richards, who was kind enough to buy me a Jack Daniel's one night at a James Brown concert at the Apollo Theater and discuss with me the finer (and not so finer) points of playing with Chuck Berry; and Bobby Keys, who was a very welcome guest on my radio show, and too much of a Texas gentleman to dish on the Stones ("the Stones" meaning "Mick") while we were on the air, but stuck around to make an afternoon of getting high on Old Fashioneds and charmed me with his version of events. I should also mention that I bumped into Ronnie Wood one afternoon at the taping of a Jerry Lee Lewis television special while he was waiting for his turn to sit in. I told him it was good to see him, and he pumped my hand enthusiastically and told me, "Yeah, man, good to see you, too, how have you been?" which reminded me that ninety percent of being famous is pretending to remember all of the people you have met before. We had never met, of course, but it was nice of him to remember me anyway.

Before writing this, that was the sum of my personal contact with the Stones—not bad, really, drinking with Keith and Bobby Keys, and getting to admire the amazing job Ronnie's colorist did on his enduring vertical explosion of hair, which was so black that it seemed like the sort of thing that Stephen Hawking used to write about. No light could escape his coif. It was like a cosmic anomaly.

And then something even more remarkable happened—Charlie Watts called me on the phone. It was early in the morning in New York, he was calling from England during the pandemic, and he left me a message: "Hi, you don't know me, my name is Charlie Watts, I want to thank you for writing this lovely book, and for having Charlie Parker on your voice mail." Which itself was incredible—in the twenty years of having the same outgoing message (it just happened to be what I was listening to when I got my first flip phone, and it stuck), Charlie Watts is the only one who has ever recognized it. I called him back right away, of course, and we talked about this and that for a few minutes, and he invited me to come see him when the Stones got back out on the road. I thought maybe I was being pranked—not probable, but also not impossible considering the clowns I know—so I asked him *a secret drummer's question* and he passed with flying colors. For now, at least, I'll keep the high sign between Charlie and me, but he was very sweet and as unerringly polite as you would imagine, and the entire experience was like having your hand shaken firmly by someone wearing a velvet glove.

When it came to making this book a reality—I have probably been thinking about it since I was fifteen, about twenty-five years before I wrote my first book, and about ten years hence—John Cerullo at Backbeat shared my enthusiasm immediately. I thank John for his spirit and publishing expertise, and for leading an excellent team, including Clare Cerullo, who has had my back through the entire process of turning my thoughts into ink on paper.

Katherine Barner provided outstanding editorial assistance.

Tom Seabrook was a great partner on both the editorial and design fronts, two talents that are not always found in the same person. If this book looks good and makes any sense at all, Tom had a great hand in it.

Tilman Reitzle, who has done so many wonderful book covers and has helped me out with gig flyers, posters, CD covers, and more, is my go-to guy in the art department. He scribbled the handwritten lettering on the cover, and worked with me with rare patience, as he always does, to get the energy of the thing just right.

It was a rare treat listening to the Rolling Stones with ace session man and snare-drum superstar Kenny Aranoff, who helped me get deep inside the stylings of Charlie Watts, and wrote out the cool micro-drum charts within to give this volume a little extra *zork*. Kenny has sat behind Paul McCartney, Iggy Pop, Bob Dylan, Meat Loaf, Stevie Nicks, John Fogerty … the list is endless. Kenny has also played with the Rolling Stones, adding some percussion to *Bridges to Babylon*, and with Charlie Watts on his project with Jim Keltner.[1] Never mind his luminous bona

---

1 Kenny was also invited to play on a Mick Jagger solo tour, and got as far as a studio jam session, but ultimately had scheduling conflicts. Mick always chose A-list session guys for his band, but to get an invitation from Charlie meant you were *Charlie approved.*

fides, Kenny is a drummer's drummer and a true mensch, generous, honest, and very funny. While we were marveling over Charlie's incredibly weird and wonderful blurt of a drum intro on "Hang Fire," Kenny said, "I wish I were in the Stones—no one else would ever let me play like that!"

Thanks to photographer Ethan Russell, who was on tour with the Stones in '69 and '72, and was a pleasure to work with. Also thanks to Derek Davidson at Photofest, who was a great asset when it came to digging into the wonders and absurdities of this mess.

A very special thank-you to Don McAulay—Charlie's drum technician, my man inside the castle walls, and as nice a guy as you'll ever meet in this bloody racket—for his unfiltered ardor and kindness, and for getting my book into his boss's hands (and quite a few others). One of the best things about writing a book is making new friends, and Don is tops.

Ditto, I must thank John DeChristopher, a gentleman and true believer whose enthusiasm for the first edition of this book helped put it in front of the like-minded and miscreant—drummers who read are surely a breed apart.

Add to this elite list Dee Pop, a great friend, a rabbi and scholar when it comes to the art of drumming, a *sensei* wise enough to never stop being a student, who has played with everyone from Odetta and Chuck Berry to the Gun Club and the Clash, not to mention powering his long running band the Bush Tetras (and moonlighting with me in the Edison Rocket Train). His swift embrace of this book let me know early on that I had nothing to fear from prickly *musicos* clutching their pearls—I probably deserve a few minutes in the penalty box for unnecessary roughness, but I always come in hot. Like Charlie, and Keith, and a few others, I'll leave the bullshit for the punters

Undying thanks to the many musicians who have played with me over the years, and have helped me turn every reading and signing into real beat happenings—and twist the audio book of this rant into a new strain of pure literary mayhem—but especially the World's Greatest Piano Player, Mickey Finn; Beatnik No. 1, Bob Bert; Jon "The Hitman" Spencer; and "The Count," Peter Zaremba. Thanks to the twin guitars of the Second Greatest Rock'n'Roll Band in the World, the Lucille Balls (Keith Streng! Mike Giblin!), and to the folks who genuinely keep the fire burning in New York City, in good times and bad, and were essential to launching this book with both roll and rock—the indefatigable Jesse Malin (who has generously been the man-behind-the-screen for every East Village *book mitzvah* I've been fortunate enough to celebrate), and the unsinkable Diane Gentile. Thank you.

Lastly, but certainly not leastly, thanks to the brilliant and beautiful Christine "Daisy" Martin, who puts up with me on a daily basis, which is no Swiss picnic, even though I'm not allowed to set up my drums in our Brooklyn apartment. I guess some day I'm going to have to buy us a house.

Maysles, Jagger, Maysles, and Watts, Gimme Shelter, *1970.* (Allstar Picture Library Ltd./Alamy)

SELECT BIBLIOGRAPHY

A complete discography lies far beyond the scope of this simple work, and would have to include not only the entirety of the Rolling Stones' recorded output (including bootlegs and dozens of live recordings and videos), but also the complete discographies of Led Zeppelin, the Who, the Beatles, Elvis Presley, Jimmy Reed, Sun Records, Chess Records, Motown, etc, etc., not to mention the collected works of the many musicians, and particularly drummers, mentioned within. Specific albums and songs are mentioned in the text, and extended playlists covering the entire book are available for streaming at www.mikeedison.com.

The quote that makes up half of the epigraph of this book was taken from Jas Obrecht's complete interview with Charlie Watts, conducted in 1994, for an authorized Rolling Stones one-shot magazine, *Inside the Voodoo Lounge*.

Abelson, Danny. "50 & Counting: Sonic Truth for the Rolling Stones Latest Tour." *Live Sound*. July 15, 2013.

Altham, Keith. "The Rolling Stone Charlie Watts Takes Over Mansion of First Archbishop of Canterbury!" *New Musical Express*, January 20, 1968.

Berry, Chuck. *Chuck Berry: The Autobiography*. New York: Harmony Books, 1987.

Beuttler, Bill. "The Charlie Watts Interview." *DownBeat*, February 1987.

"Bill Wyman Charlie Watts Rolling Stones Interview 1976 Tour." Youtube. Video File. June 23, 2012. www.youtube.com.

Blanchard, Wayne. "19 Reasons to Love Charlie Watts." *Drum!*, April 12, 2017.

Borgerson, Bruce. "The 'Brown Sugar' Sessions: Jimmy Johnson on Recording the Rolling Stones." *Tape Op*, November/December 2001.

Bungey, John. "Charlie Watts: Me, Retire? What Am I Gonna Do? Mow the Lawn?" *The Times*, May 5, 2017.

Case, Brian. "Charlie Watts Big Band: Ronnie Scott's, London." *Melody Maker*, November 30, 1985.

Charlie Is My Darling. Directed by Peter Whitehead. 1966.

Cocksucker Blues. Directed by Robert Frank. 1972.

Crossfire Hurricane. Directed by Brett Morgen. 2012. HBO.

DeCurtis, Anthony. "Keith Richards: A Stone Alone Comes Clean." *Rolling Stone*, October 6, 1988.

DeCurtis, Anthony. "Steel Wheels." *Rolling Stone*, August 29, 1989.

DeCurtis, Anthony. "The Rolling Stone Interview: Keith Richards." *Rolling Stone*, October 6, 1988.

Derogatis, Jim. "Q&A: Charlie Watts on His New Jazz Album, Sketching Hotel Beds, and the 40-Year-Old Sex Pistols." *Rolling Stone*, May 30, 1996.

Doyle, Patrick. "Keith Richards on Getting Busted, Zeppelin and Stones' Future." *Rolling Stone*, October 8, 2015.

Egan, Sean. *Keith Richards on Keith Richards: Interviews and Encounters*. Chicago: Chicago Review Press, 2013.

Eggar, Robin. "Charlie Watts: The Esquire Interview." *Esquire*, June 1998.

Ellen, Barbara. "Charlie Watts: Proper Charlie." *The Observer*, July 9, 2000.

Erlewine, Michael. "Odie Payne, Jr." *AllMusic*. www.allmusic.com.

Falzerano, Chet. *Charlie Watts' Favorite Drummers*. Anaheim: Centerstream Publishing, 2017.

"The First Years of Disco (1972–1974)." *Disco Savvy*. www.discosavvy.com.

Fish, Scott K. "Fred Below—Magic Maker." *Modern Drummer*, September 1983.

Fish, Scott K. and Max Weinberg. "A Conversation With Charlie Watts." *Modern Drummer*, August/September 1982.

Flanagan, Bill. "Q&A with Bill Flanagan." *Bob Dylan*. March 22, 2017. www.bobdylan.com.

Flans, Robyn. "Charlie Watts." *Modern Drummer*, August/September 1982.

Fletcher, Tony. *Moon: The Life and Death of a Rock Legend*. New York: Spike, 1999.

Flippo, Chet. "The Rolling Stones Grow Old Angrily." *Rolling Stone*, August 21, 1980.

Fornatale, Peter. *50 Licks: Myths and Stories from Half a Century of the Rolling Stones*. New York: Bloomsbury USA, 2013.

Fortnam, Ian. "Interview: Keith Richards and Charlie Watts on the Rolling Stones in Exile." *Classic Rock*, November 15, 2016.

Fricke, David. "Q&A: Charlie Watts." *Rolling Stone*, November 22, 2005.

From the Vault—Hyde Park—Live in 1969. 1969. Eagle Rock Entertainment DVD.

From the Vault—L.A. Forum—Live in 1975. 1975. Eagle Vision DVD.

Giles, Jeff. "That Time the Rolling Stones Regrouped for 'Steel Wheels.'" *Ultimate Classic Rock*, August 29, 2015.

Giles, Jeff. "When the Wheels Came Off: The History of the Rolling Stones 'Dirty Work.'" *Ultimate Classic Rock*, May 9, 2014.

Gimme Shelter. Directed by Albert Maysles, David Maysles, and Charlotte Zwerin. 1970. Maysles Films.

Gray, Tyler. "The Making of the Rolling Stones' 'Exile on Main Street.'" *New York Post*, May 9, 2010.

Greenfield, Robert. *Exile on Main Street*. Da Capo Press, 2008.

Greenfield, Robert. "The Rolling Stone Interview: Keith Richards." *Rolling Stone*, August 19, 1971.

Harper, Simon. "Charlie Watts on 'Exile On Main Street.'" *Clash*, May 19, 2010.

Hudson, Scott. "Rock and Walk: Rolling Stones' 'Dirty Work.'" *Argus Leader*, June 30, 2014.

Ingham, Chris. "Ten Questions for Charlie Watts." *Mojo*, July, 1996.

Jefferson, Margo. "Ellington Beyond Category." *The New York Times*, October 15, 1993.

Jisi, Chris. "Partners In Time: John Entwistle & Keith Moon." *DRUM!*, August 23, 2013.

Johns, Glyn. *Sound Man: A Life Recording Hits with the Rolling Stones, the Who, Led Zeppelin, the Eagles , Eric Clapton, the Faces ...* New York: Plume, 2014.

"'Just Another Band to Me': In a Rare Talk, Charlie Watts Remembers Joining the Rolling Stones." *Something Else!*, December 13, 2013.

Kaufman, Spencer. "10 Things You Didn't Know About Charlie Watts." *Ultimate Classic Rock*, June 2, 2011.

Kelley, Ken. "That Time Mick Jagger Kicked Off His First Solo Tour." *Ultimate Classic Rock*, March 16, 2016.

Kubernik, Harvey. "Engineer Andy Johns Discusses the Making of the Rolling Stones' 'Exile on Main Street.'" *Goldmine*, May 8, 2010.

Ladies and Gentlemen: The Rolling Stones. Directed by Rollin Binzer. 1994. Dragonaire Ltd.

Let's Spend the Night Together. Directed by Hal Ashby. 1983.

Loder, Kurt. "Keith Richards: The Rolling Stone 20th Anniversary Interview." *Rolling Stone*, November 5, 1987.

Margotin, Philippe and Jean-Michel Guesdon. *The Rolling Stones All the Songs: The Story Behind Every Track*. New York: Black Dog & Leventhal, 2016.

Merlis, Jim. "Rolling Stones Producer Jimmy Miller: 15 Things You Didn't Know." *Rolling Stone*, May 24, 2018.

Mojo Staff. "Charlie Watts: 'I Thought the Stones Were Just Another Band.'" *Mojo*, July 3, 2015.

Needham, Alex. "The Rolling Stones: 'We Are Theatre and Reality at the Same Time.'" *The Guardian*, December 1, 2016.

Newey, Jon. "The Beat Goes On: Charlie Watts and the Great Jazz Drummers." *Jazzwise*, July 2000.

Palmer, Alun. "'I Drank Too Much and Took Drugs. I Went Mad Really': Charlie Watts, the Calm Man of the Rolling Stones, Looks Back at 50 Years of Chaos." *Mirror*, July 12, 2012.

Patoski, Joe Nick. "Watching Willie's Back." *Oxford American*, Winter 2014.

Paytress, Mark. "The MOJO Interview." *Mojo*, August 2015.

Pidgeon, John. "The Back Line: Bill Wyman and Charlie Watts." *Creem*, November 1978.

Remnick, David. "Groovin' High." *The New Yorker*, October 25, 2010.

Richards, Keith and James Fox. *Life*. New York: Back Bay Books, 2011.

The Rolling Stones. *According to the Rolling Stones*. San Francisco: Chronicle Books LLC, 2003.

The Rolling Stones: Havana Moon. Directed by Paul Dugdale. 2016. Eagle Rock Entertainment.

The Rolling Stones: Some Girls Live. Directed by Lynn Leneau Calmes. 2011. Eagle Rock Entertainment.

Sandall, Robert. "Charlie Watts: The Rock." *Mojo*, May 1994.

Schlueter, Brad. "Analysis of the Trickiest Drum Intros on Record." *DRUM!*, November 21, 2012.

Shine a Light. Directed by Martin Scorsese. 2008. Paramount Classics.

"Somebody Explain Charlie Watts to Me." *Straight Dope Message Board*. June 10, 2008. https://boards.straightdope.com.

"Stones' Wood: I Did So Many Drugs, Keith Richards Got Mad!" *Daily News*, October 15, 2007.

Sweeting, Adam. "Charlie Watts: I've Recorded Drums in the Lavatory." *Telegraph*, March 14, 2012.

Terich, Jeff. "History's Greatest Monsters: The Rolling Stones— Dirty Work." *Treble*, March 22, 2013.

Thompson, Dave. *I Hate New Music: The Classic Rock Manifesto*. New York: Backbeat, 2008.

Tingen, Paul. "Secrets of the Mix Engineers: Bob Clearmountain." *Sound on Sound*, February 2009.

Vaillancourt, Eric. "Rock 'n' Roll in the 1950s: Rockin' for Civil Rights," (Master's Thesis, University of New York College at Brockport, 2011).

Varga, George. "Rolling Stones Flashback: Charlie Watts Interview." *San Diego Union Tribune*, May 19, 2015.

Watts, Charlie. "Home Entertainment." *The Guardian*, May 31, 2001.

Wenner, Jann S. "Mick Jagger Remembers." *Rolling Stone*, December 14, 1995.

Wood, Ronnie. *Ronnie: The Autobiography*. New York: St. Martin's Press, 2007.

Woodall, James. "Ringo's No Joke. He Was a Genius and the Beatles Were Lucky to Have Him." *The Spectator*, July 4, 2015.

"The World's 'Luckiest' Drummers?" *The Rush Forum*. September 5, 2012. www.therushforum.com.

Wyman, Bill. *Stone Alone: The Story of a Rock 'n' Roll Band*. New York: Viking Adult, 1990.

Zoro and Daniel Glass. *The Commandments of Early Rhythm and Blues Drumming*. Van Nuys: Alfred Publishing Company, 2008.

INDEX

ABOUT THE AUTHOR

MIKE EDISON is a genuine rock'n'roll renaissance man. He is the former editor and publisher of famed cannabis magazine *High Times*, and was the editor-in-chief of the courageously irresponsible *Screw*. He is the author of twenty-eight "adult" novels, and an internationally known musician who spent much of the 1980s and '90s seeing the world from behind a drum set, opening for bands as diverse as Sonic Youth, Soundgarden, and the Ramones. He has written extensive liner notes for, among others, Iggy Pop and the Jon Spencer Blues Explosion, and has contributed to numerous magazines and websites, including *Huffington Post*, the *Daily Beast*, the *New York Observer*, *Spin* (writing about the Rolling Stones), *Interview*, and *New York Press*, for which he covered classical music and professional wrestling.

His most recent books have included the highly praised memoirs *I Have Fun Everywhere I Go* and *You Are a Complete Disappointment*, as well as the sprawling social history of sex on the newsstand, *Dirty! Dirty! Dirty!*, written during his time as a writer-in-residence at the New York Public Library. He also writes prolifically about food and wine, notably collaborating with restaurateur and viniculturist Joe Bastianich on his *New York Times* bestselling memoir, *Restaurant Man*, of which writer Bret Easton Ellis has said, "The directness and energy have a cinematic rush ... not a single boring sentence."

Edison can frequently be seen with his long-running blues, gospel, and garage-punk experiment The Edison Rocket Train, and he speaks frequently on free speech, sex, drugs, and the American counterculture. He is "proof positive that one can be both edgy and erudite, lowbrow and literate, and take joy in the unbridled pleasures of the id without sacrificing the higher mind." (PopMatters.com)

Edison lives and works in Brooklyn, NY. Please visit him at www.mikeedison.com.